T0338546

COMPUTATIONAL GEOMETRY
with Independent
and Dependent Uncertainties

COMPUTATIONAL GEOMETRY

with Independent and Dependent Uncertainties

Rivka Gitik

The Hebrew University of Jerusalem, Israel

Leo Joskowicz

The Hebrew University of Jerusalem, Israel

World Scientific

NEW JERSEY · LONDON · SINGAPORE · BEIJING · SHANGHAI · HONG KONG · TAIPEI · CHENNAI · TOKYO

Published by

World Scientific Publishing Co. Pte. Ltd.

5 Toh Tuck Link, Singapore 596224

USA office: 27 Warren Street, Suite 401-402, Hackensack, NJ 07601

UK office: 57 Shelton Street, Covent Garden, London WC2H 9HE

Library of Congress Cataloging-in-Publication Data

Names: Gitik, Rivka, author. | Joskowicz, Leo, 1961–   author.

Title: Computational geometry with independent and dependent uncertainties /
    Rivka Gitik (the Hebrew University of Jerusalem, Israel),
    Leo Joskowicz (the Hebrew University of Jerusalem, Israel).

Description: New Jersey : World Scientific, [2023] | Includes bibliographical references and index.

Identifiers: LCCN 2022021777 | ISBN 9789811253836 (hardcover) |
    ISBN 9789811253843 (ebook) | ISBN 9789811253850 (ebook)

Subjects: LCSH: Geometry--Data processing. | Computer algorithms.

Classification: LCC QA448.D38 G58 2023 | DDC 516.00285--dc23/eng20220630

LC record available at https://lccn.loc.gov/2022021777

British Library Cataloguing-in-Publication Data

A catalogue record for this book is available from the British Library.

For any available supplementary material, please visit
https://www.worldscientific.com/worldscibooks/10.1142/12765#t=suppl

Desk Editors: Balasubramanian Shanmugam/Steven Patt

Typeset by Stallion Press
Email: enquiries@stallionpress.com

Printed in Singapore

I dedicate this book to my parents, Michael and Ruth, and to Emmanuel with love.

— Rivka

I dedicate this book to the memory of my parents, Alfredo and Esther, to my beloved daughters, Yael and Dana, and to my very dear Leah.

— Leo

Preface

Geometric uncertainty is ubiquitous in mechanical CAD/CAM, robotics, computer vision, wireless networks and many other fields. Sensing, localization, measurement and manufacturing processes are intrinsically imprecise, and thereby introduce error and uncertainty. In contrast, the corresponding geometric models are usually exact and do not account for these inaccuracies. Modeling and computing geometric variability and its consequences are thus of great scientific, technical and economic importance.

This book presents LPGUM (Linear Parametric Geometric Uncertainty Model), a parametric model for representing geometric entities with dependent uncertainties between them. LPGUM allows the systematic study of geometric uncertainty and its related algorithms. In this model, basic geometric features, such as coordinates, points, lines and arcs, are defined by a common set of parameters with uncertainty intervals. The uncertainty zones around nominal feature locations are defined by uncertainty sensitivity matrices whose entries indicate the coordinates' sensitivity to parameter variations and their dependencies. The sensitivity matrices are derived from the functional relations between the design or measurement parameters by taking the partial derivative of the function for each parameter at the nominal value. The sensitivity matrices allow modeling of the full range of uncertainty dependency and parameter coupling, from independence through partial dependency, to complete dependency.

The book formalizes the concept of geometric uncertainty with dependencies and presents efficient algorithms to solve four key problems: (1) compute the envelope of uncertain lines and circles;

(2) answer geometric half-plane retrieval queries of points in the plane, including exact and uncertain point sets and half-plane queries defined by an exact or uncertain line; (3) construct the Euclidean Minimum Spanning Tree (EMST) of a set of uncertain points, test its stability and compute its total weight; (4) construct the Voronoi diagram (VD) and Delaunay triangulation (DT) of a set of uncertain points, test their stability, compute their components, answer exact and uncertain point location queries in a stable uncertain VD and dynamically update it.

The main contribution of this book is the model which allows for describing and efficiently handling geometric objects with dependent uncertainty. We show that the model is expressive and that the additional computational cost for allowing for dependent uncertainty using this model is in most cases a low polynomial multiplicative term.

About the Authors

Rivka Gitik is a Lecturer at the Open University of Israel and an algorithm developer in a major medical imaging company. She holds a Ph.D. degree in Computer Science from the Hebrew University of Jerusalem, Israel, and a B.A. degree in Computer Science and Economic from the Open University.

Leo Joskowicz is a Professor at the School of Computer Science and Engineering, the Hebrew University of Jerusalem, Israel, and is the Founder and Director of the Computer Aided Surgery and Medical Image Processing Laboratory (CASMIP Lab). He is a Fellow of the American Society of Mechanical Engineers (ASME), the Institute of Electrical and Electronic Engineers (IEEE) and the Medical Image Computing and Computer Assisted Intervention Society (MICCAI). He is the co-author of the book *The Configuration Space Method for Kinematic Design of Mechanisms* (MIT Press, 2010) and of over 250 peer-reviewed papers in Computational Geometry, Mechanism Design, Medical Robotics, Medical Image Analysis and Computer Aided Surgery. He is the recipient of the

2010 Maurice E. Muller Award for Excellence in Computer Assisted Surgery by the International Society of Computer Aided Orthopaedic Surgery (CAOS) and the 2007 Kaye Innovation Award. He holds a Ph.D. degree in Computer Science from the Courant Institute of Mathematical Sciences, New York University, USA.

Acknowledgments

Yaron Ostrovsky-Berman, Yoni Myers and Or Bartal participated in the earlier stages of the research that led to this book. Their contributions appear in the bibliography and are documented in the publications under their names. The cover design is based on an original drawing by Dana Joskowicz.

Contents

Chapter 1

Introduction

Geometric uncertainty is ubiquitous in mechanical CAD/CAM, robotics, computer vision, wireless networks and many other fields. Sensing, localization, measurement and manufacturing processes are intrinsically imprecise, and thereby introduce error and uncertainty. In contrast, the corresponding geometric models are usually exact and do not account for these inaccuracies. Modeling and computing geometric variability and its consequences are thus of great scientific, technical and economic importance.

This book presents a model for handling elementary geometric objects with uncertainty in their location and shape. This model can be used to solve classical computational geometry problems in which objects have uncertainties. The unique feature of the model is that it allows dependencies between the geometric uncertainties of the objects and their relationships.

This chapter consists of five sections. Section 1.1 provides the background and motivation. Section 1.2 describes the problem and presents a survey of the relevant literature. Section 1.3 presents the goals of this book. Section 1.4 outlines the advantages and the novelty of the book. Section 1.5 states the organization of the book.

1.1 Background

Geometric retrieval and the computation of Euclidean minimum spanning tree (EMST), Voronoi diagram (VD), Delaunay triangulation (DT) and related structures of points in the plane in the presence of geometric uncertainty are problems of great theoretical and practical importance. In many situations, the point locations cannot be determined exactly, so modeling their location uncertainty is required to understand their variability and the stability of their spatial relationships.

A variety of models and representations have been proposed to model geometric uncertainty of elementary geometric entities, e.g., points, lines and circles, and of composite geometric entities, e.g., convex hulls (CHs), VD, DT and EMST. The frameworks can be divided into two broad categories: deterministic and probabilistic.

Deterministic frameworks model geometric uncertainty by describing the instances and the regions in which the uncertain geometric entities are located. Probabilistic frameworks model geometric uncertainty by assigning a probability distribution to the geometric entities and to their locations. In the deterministic framework, the most common approach is to model point location uncertainty with a region that bounds the point coordinates' variability. Regions are simple geometric entities, e.g., line segments [1,2], rectangles [3], squares [1,4], circles or disks [1,4], or convex polygons [5,6]. Deterministic geometric variations can be modeled by allowing the location parameters of the geometric entities to vary within specified intervals, called tolerances [7–9]. Related frameworks include perturbation analysis, ε-geometry and functional sensitivity analysis [10,11]. The advantage of the deterministic approach is that it allows the exact geometric analysis of location uncertainty, thereby providing a worst-case analysis of the geometric uncertainty. In contrast, in the probabilistic approach, sets of points are constructed by randomly drawing each point with an independent probability and deriving the statistical and geometric properties of the resulting point sets. A central question in both frameworks is determining the topological stability of uncertain geometric structures: Given a set of points whose locations are uncertain, determine if the topology of the structure is the same for all possible point locations [12].

A key limitation of nearly all existing geometric uncertainty models is that they do not account for dependencies between the point location uncertainties. The dependencies, induced by the problem specifications, are frequent in engineering and in practical applications. Ignoring the dependencies between geometric uncertainties often results in an overestimation of the location uncertainty, in an incorrect classification or in an incorrect topological stability

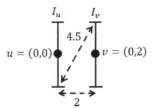

Fig. 1.1. Simple example that illustrates that ignoring the dependency of two points u and v (black points) overestimates the distance between them. The vertical solid lines are the location uncertainty of u and v. The lines are of length 4. In dotted arrows are the maximum and the minimum distance between u and v when the point uncertainties are independent.

determination. We illustrate next geometric uncertainty dependencies with a simple example (Fig. 1.1).

Let $u = (0,0)$ and $v = (2,0)$ be two points in the plane and let their location uncertainty be 2 units in each direction in the y coordinate, i.e., the possible locations of the points (point instances) lie in vertical intervals I_u and I_v of length 4 units. When the point uncertainties are independent, the minimum and maximum distances between u and v are 2 and $\sqrt{20} \approx 4.5$ units, respectively. Assume now that the location uncertainties of u and v are dependent (coupled), so that when the location of u changes, the location of v changes in the same direction and at the same rate. In this case, the minimum and maximum distance between u and v is always 2 units. Ignoring the dependency between the location uncertainties of u and v overestimates the maximum distance between them by $4.5/2 = 2.25$ times.

1.2 Literature Review

We present next an overview of existing models for handling imprecise geometry and related work.

In recent years, efforts have been made to provide a good model for handling geometric uncertainty. These efforts have been carried out in many fields ranging from Mechanical Engineering to Computer Science. Next, we first review the literature related to the deterministic and probabilistic models. We review next works on topological stability. Finally, we present an overview of previous work on the

Linear Parametric Geometric Uncertainty Model (LPGUM), which is the basis of this book.

1.2.1 Deterministic models

Deterministic approaches model point location uncertainty by defining a few parameters and relations whose variations define the set of possible point locations.

Related geometric retrieval problems for half-plane point retrieval in the presence of uncertainty are location queries, set membership classification and range queries. Arya and Mount [13] describe an approximate range query model in which queries are specified by a bounded range Q of diameter w and an approximation parameter $\varepsilon > 0$. Points whose distance from the boundary of Q is $\leq \varepsilon w$ are labeled as uncertain. Another approach is to model point uncertainty with moving points whose locations are time sampled [14, 15]. The main disadvantage of these methods is that they cannot model dependencies between point locations.

More broadly, geometric uncertainty has been modeled as sensitivity with linear parametric dependencies. Ben-Tal *et al.* [16] describe methods for robust optimization, a methodology for handling optimization problems with uncertain data. Their model and motivation is similar to ours, as it seeks the worst-case characterization of linearly coupled uncertainties. However, their research focuses on robust optimization and does not address the geometric and topological aspects of the problems. In particular, no formulation and solutions for the uncertain half-plane, EMST, VD and DT problems are presented.

Various deterministic approaches for computing VDs and DTs with point location uncertainties have been proposed in the literature. Löffler and Snoeyink [17] describe an $O\left(n \log n\right)$ time algorithm to preprocess a set of n disjoint unit disks whose center coordinates are exact and an $O\left(n\right)$ time algorithm for computing the DT of points selected inside each disk. Devillers [18] describe an algorithm to compute the DT of n disjoint unit disks in expected $O(n)$ time after expected $O\left(n \log n\right)$ time preprocessing. Buchin *et al.* [19] describe algorithms to compute the DT of point sets whose location uncertainty is bounded by overlapping disks of different sizes and by fat regions. McAllister *et al.* [5] describe an algorithm for computing a VD instance of k disjoint convex sets of n points in $O\left(nk \log nk\right)$

time. Other related work includes linear time construction algorithms for the ε-geometry model [10, 11], in which the point location uncertainty is a disk of radius ε. The drawback of this model is that ε is small and that it is the same for all points.

1.2.2 Probabilistic models

Probabilistic approaches model point location uncertainty by associating a probability density function around each nominal point location [20]. For example, a range query on a set of uncertain points returns points whose probability of being in the range is above a predefined threshold. Chen and Cheng [21] study the efficiency of queries that return probabilistic guarantees for location data with uncertainty. Agarwal *et al.* [22] study range queries in which the point location uncertainty is modeled with a probability density function. Given a query interval and a probability threshold, their algorithm reports all the points that are inside the interval with the specified probability. Kamousi *et al.* [23,24] describe a stochastic model in which random sets of n points in d-dimensional Euclidean space are constructed by drawing each point with a random independent probability p. They present solutions for the closest pair, closest point in VD and EMST problems. Fink *et al.* [25] describe an $O(n^d)$ time algorithm for computing the probability that two d-dimensional stochastic point sets are linearly separable. Xue and Li [26] investigate the problem of computing the probability that a realization of a set of n colored stochastic points in R^d contains inter-color dominances.

Agarwal *et al.* [27] propose a model in which the point locations' uncertainties are described by independent probability distributions over a finite number of possible locations, including a null location to account for non-existence of the point. They describe an algorithm for computing the probabilistic CH of a set of points in this model. Suri *et al.* [28] study the problem of finding the CH with the maximum occurrence probability in a stochastic point location model. Pérez-Lantero [29] describes an algorithm for computing the probabilistic CH of a random set of points drawn from a probability distribution function.

The main drawbacks of probabilistic models are that the point location probability functions are usually assumed to be symmetric and isotropic, that they do not account for dependencies between the probabilities and that they always underestimate the worst-case geometric variability.

1.2.3   Topological stability

The topological stability of EMST, VD, DT and related structures of uncertain points has been widely studied. Most works on stability focus on small point location perturbations, e.g., floating point errors and small deviations. Jaromczyk and Wasilkowski [30] present a numerically stable algorithm for computing the CH of a set of points in the floating-point arithmetic model. Fortune [31,32] studies the correctness of CH and DT computation with approximate arithmetic over the reals. Ely and Leclerc [33] present a robust in-circle test algorithm that models points as small disks and avoids round-off errors common to rational and large integer arithmetic.

A related question is that of determining how much the point locations can be perturbed while preserving the topological stability of their structures. Abellanas *et al.* [34] and Boissonnat *et al.* [35] study the conditions under which the DT of points whose locations is perturbed by a small ε and retains their structure. Li and Milenkovic [36] study the problem of strongly CHs using rounded arithmetic. In this model, a convex polygon P is a ϵ-strongly convex δ-hull iff P remains convex when no point lies farther than δ outside P when its vertices' locations are perturbed by up to ϵ. Evans and Sember [37] investigate the structure of DT in which point location uncertainty is modeled by a disk and describe an optimal algorithm for computing the edges that are guaranteed to exist in every DT. Weller [9] studies the problem of computing a bound on the distance that points of a VD can be moved without changing their Voronoi neighborhood structure. Reem [38] studies the relation between small point location perturbations and their effect on their Voronoi cells. He shows that the effect remains small in uniformly convex normed spaces when there is a common lower bound on the pairwise point distance. Goberna and de Serio [39] study the stability of VD cells in which some point locations are uncertain. They analyze the effect of small location perturbations of subsets of points on their corresponding cells. All these works assume that the point location uncertainties are small, isotropic and independent. None model stability in the presence of dependencies.

For deterministic geometric models that model point location uncertainty with simple geometric entities, Löffler and van Kreveld [3] prove that for a set of arbitrarily sized and oriented possibly intersecting line segments, the problem of choosing a point on each segment such that the area or diameter of the resulting CH is as large as possible is NP-hard.

A geometric model that accounts for dependencies between point locations are kinetic models and their data structures. In a kinetic model, the point locations are time dependent, i.e. points move with a pre-defined speed and trajectory, so their location is known at all times. In this model, Meulemans *et al.* [40] define a geometric algorithm to be stable when small time-dependent changes in the input result in small changes in the output. They introduce an analysis framework that allows for three types of stability analysis, event stability, topological stability and Lipschitz stability, and demonstrate this framework by applying it to kinetic EMST. Agarwal *et al.* [41,42] define a stable Delaunay graph as a dynamic DT subgraph that undergoes few or no topological changes and that retains useful DT properties, e.g., minimum angles between edges. They prove that the upper bound on the number of topological changes in the DT of points moving in the plane is nearly cubic in the number of points [41]. Albers *et al.* [43] extend this result to n points moving along a given trajectory in d-dimensional Euclidean space. As the points move, their VD changes continuously, causing the VD structure to change at critical moments. They show that there are at most $O(n^d \lambda_s(n))$ topological events, where $\lambda_s(n)$ is the nearly linear maximum length of a (n, s)-Davenport–Schinzel sequence and s is a constant that depends on the point motions. The key drawback of using kinetic data structures to model location dependencies is that the point locations' uncertainties all depend on a single common parameter, time. Independent, partially dependent and dependent uncertainties with more parameters cannot be accounted for in this model.

Nearest neighbor queries in the presence of uncertainty have also been studied. Xie *et al.* [44] use the VD to answer nearest neighbor queries for uncertain spatial databases. In the probabilistic approach, Iijima and Ishikawa [45] describe algorithms to answer nearest neighbor queries in which query location uncertainty is specified by a Gaussian distribution. Ali *et al.* [46] propose the probabilistic VD for processing nearest neighbor queries on uncertain data.

Arya *et al.* [47] describe a data structure for approximate nearest neighbor queries with a (t, ε) approximate VD. In this VD, space is partitioned into constant complexity cells in which each cell is associated with t points whose nearest neighbor is within a distance factor of at most $(1 + \varepsilon)$. A query retrieves the most probable nearest neighbor. Suri and Verbeek [48] study nearest neighbor search in a stochastic point set. The drawback of probabilistic models is that they may miss points and that they do not account for dependencies between the probabilities.

1.2.4   The linear parametric geometric uncertainty model

The LPGUM is an expressive and computationally efficient worst-case, first-order linear approximation of geometric uncertainty that supports parametric dependencies between point locations [49–56]. The advantages of parametric models over geometric ones are their compactness, uniformity, and mathematical and computational properties. LPGUM is general and expressive, and allows for parameter dependencies typical of tolerance specifications and metrology. Myers and Joskowicz [54] describe the basic properties of uncertainty zones of points and lines in the plane and in space in LPGUM and show that their time complexity is low-polynomial in the number of dependent parameters. This led to efficient algorithms for computing uncertainty zones of points, lines and circles [54], for relative point orientation, for point set distance problems and for uncertain range queries [53], and for topological stability and CH computation [49] in the LPGUM.

The LPGUM is motivated by the theory and practice of metrology and tolerancing in Mechanical Engineering [57]. Tolerancing models establish the location and shape variability of parts in a mechanical assembly. Two types of worst-case tolerance analysis methods have been developed. Sampling-based methods define key characteristics (e.g., clearance, fitting and alignment) in terms of the part geometries, and then analyze the sensitivity to variations by sampling selected or random instances of the part geometries. Since the features are constrained to remain within their tolerance zones, the domain of the tolerance parameters is typically a high-dimensional convex polytope. While general, these methods are computationally intensive and can miss important configurations.

Geometry-based methods strive to compute the parts' uncertainty zone. Methods based on offsetting operations and vertex bounding volumes derive the minimum part tolerance zones which contain all the part instances that meet the specifications. However, the part and tolerancing models do not model coupling and dependencies between parameters, which are the norm in tolerancing chains. They are often too simplistic for realistic applications. Other models require specialized procedures for every type of feature and incorporate *ad hoc* simplifying assumptions that preclude quantifying the approximation error. See [51,55] for a detailed discussion of these issues.

1.3 Goals

The main goal of this book is to present a model of geometric uncertainty that is both expressive and computationally efficient. Specifically, the model should have the following properties:

1. Provide a worst-case analysis of elementary geometric entities.
2. Provide a full description of uncertain geometric entities that is not based on sampling methods.
3. Handle both dependent and independent geometric entities.
4. Have a computational complexity that is practical.

We show that the model is expressive and viable. In particular, we:

1. Provide a description of basic geometric entities using the model and show that the algorithms for computing them and their space requirements are low polynomial.
2. Demonstrate that classical computational geometry problems can be solved efficiently under the model.

1.4 Overview and Novelty

The key novelty of this book is the integration of first-order, linear geometric dependencies in an expressive and computationally efficient model. To the best of our knowledge, this is the first attempt to systematically define and derive coupled geometric uncertainties. In this model, we systematically formulate and describe efficient algorithms for a number of basic problems in Computational Geometry.

1.4.1   Uncertainty zone

We explore the basic entities of geometry under LPGUM. The uncertainty zone of an object is the union of all the points that it can occupy. The boundary of this region is called the uncertainty envelope of the object. We present new, efficient algorithms for computing uncertainty zones of lines. In addition, we determine the properties of the envelope of a three-point circle and develop an efficient algorithm for computing it for the independent case.

1.4.2   Half-plane point retrieval queries

We present efficient algorithms to answer half-plane queries. The half-plane queries we answer are as follows: Given an exact or LPGUM line defining the half-plane query and an exact or LPGUM point set, we classify the points into three disjoint sets: ABOVE, BELOW and UNCERT. Points are in ABOVE(BELOW) iff all instances of the points are above (below) all instances of the query line; otherwise, they are in UNCERT. These queries form the building blocks of other algorithms.

1.4.3   Euclidean minimum spanning trees

We address classical problems related to the EMST of uncertain point sets. We define topological stability for EMST of LPGUM points and prove that when the uncertain EMST is unstable, it may have an exponential number of topologically different instances. We describe algorithms for comparing Euclidean graph edge weights for two cases: (1) The edges do not share a common point and (2) the edges share a common point. We also describe algorithms to determine if an EMST of points is topologically stable or not. We present a definition for the weight of uncertain EMST and describe an efficient algorithm for computing the minimum and maximum weight of topological stable uncertain EMST.

1.4.4   Voronoi diagram and Delaunay triangulation

We address classical problems related to the VD and DT of uncertain point sets. The basic operation in VD and DT construction is testing if a point is inside or outside a circle defined by three points. Thus, we describe in-circle test algorithms for dependent and independent uncertainties. We define topological stability for VD of LPGUM points and we prove that when the uncertain VD is unstable, it may have an exponential number of topologically different instances. We define the LPGUM bisector, uncertain edges, vertices and faces of VD and DT and develop an algorithm for computing an LPGUM bisector for dependent and independent uncertainties. We describe algorithms for computing the vertices, edges and faces of the uncertain VD for the independent case.

We present efficient algorithms to answer point location queries in a stable uncertain VD and for dynamically updating an uncertain VD, for dependent and independent uncertainties.

1.5 Book Organization

The book consists of seven chapters and a list of references. It is organized as follows. Chapter 2 presents the LPGUM. Chapter 3 describes the properties of envelopes of points, lines and three-point circles under our model and presents efficient algorithms for computing them. Chapter 4 addresses a family of geometric half-plane retrieval queries of points in the plane in the presence of geometric uncertainty. Given an exact or LPGUM line defining the half-plane query and an exact or LPGUM point set, we describe efficient algorithms to classify the points with respect to the half-plane as always above, always below or uncertain. Chapter 5 addresses the problems of constructing the EMST of points in the plane with mutually dependent location uncertainties, testing its stability and computing its total weight. Chapter 6 addresses the problems of constructing the VD and Delaunay triangulation of points in the plane with mutually dependent location uncertainties. In this chapter, we also describe in-circle test algorithms and present algorithms to answer point location queries. Chapter 7 concludes with a summary and a list of open problems.

Chapter 2

The Linear Parametric Geometric Uncertainty Model

This chapter presents the Linear Parametric Geometric Uncertainty Model (LPGUM) and the basic LPGUM geometric entities. Section 2.1 presents basic definitions. Section 2.2 presents the LPGUM coordinate. Section 2.3 presents the LPGUM point, vector and point set. Section 2.4 presents the LPGUM line and edges. Section 2.5 presents the LPGUM three-point circle. Section 2.6 summarizes the properties and characteristics of the LPGUM.

2.1 Basic Definitions

A *parametric uncertainty model* $(q, \overline{q}, \Delta)$ is defined as follows. Let $q = (q_1, q_2, \ldots, q_k)$ be a vector of k parameters over an *uncertainty domain* Δ. Each parameter $q_j \in R$ takes a value from a bounded *uncertainty interval* $\Delta_j = [q_j^-, q_j^+]$, $q_j^- < q_j^+$ and is associated with a *nominal value* $\overline{q}_j \in R$, $\overline{q}_j \in \Delta_j$. The parameters' uncertainty domain is $\Delta = \Delta_1 \times \Delta_2 \times \cdots \times \Delta_k$. A *parameter instance* $q_a \in \Delta$ of parameter vector q is a vector in which each parameter q_j has a value in Δ_j. The *nominal parameter vector* $\overline{q} = (\overline{q}_1, \overline{q}_2, \ldots, \overline{q}_k)$ is the parameter vector value with no uncertainty.

Without loss of generality, we assume that uncertainty intervals are zero-centered symmetric, i.e., $-q_j^- = q_j^+$ and $\overline{q}_j = 0$. Asymmetric domains are transformed into symmetric ones by adjusting the

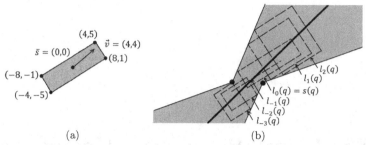

(a)   (b)

Fig. 2.1.   Uncertain point and line examples: (a) uncertain point $s(q) = (0,0)+$ $q\begin{pmatrix} 1 & -1 \\ 6 & 3 \end{pmatrix}$ and vector $\vec{v}(q) = (4,4) + q\begin{pmatrix} 1 & -1 \\ 0 & 0 \end{pmatrix}$, where $\bar{s} = (0,0)$ is the nominal point and $\vec{v} = (4,4)$ is the nominal vector. The zonotope of $s(q)$ consists of four vertices $\langle (8,1),(4,5)(-8,-1),(-4,-5)\rangle$; (b) uncertain line $l(q) = s(q)+\alpha\vec{v}(q)$ and its envelope for point $s(q)$ and vector $\vec{v}(q)$. The nominal line $\bar{l} = (0,0)+\alpha(4,4)$ is shown in black. The line envelope consists of two monotone segment chains with two segments each (outer black continuous line segments). The black dotted lines correspond to the point envelopes $l_2(q),l_1(q),l_0(q),l_{-1}(q),l_{-2}(q),l_{-3}(q)$ for the corresponding values of α. A flip event occurs at $\alpha = -1$ at which the uncertainty zone of $l_{-1}(q)$ is defined by a line segment instead of a rectangle.

nominal parameter values and uncertainty intervals:

$$q_j^{\text{mid}} = \frac{q_j^+ + q_j^-}{2}, \quad \bar{q}_j' = \bar{q}_j - q_j^{\text{mid}},$$
$$q_j'^+ = q_j^+ - q_j^{\text{mid}}, \quad q_j'^- = q_j^- - q_j^{\text{mid}}$$

For example, in Fig. 2.1(a), the parametric uncertainty model $(q,\bar{q},\Delta)$ is defined by two parameters ($k = 2$) and a vector $q = (q_1,q_2)$: parameter q_1 models the location uncertainty in the interval $\Delta_1 = [-2,2]$; parameter q_2 models the location uncertainty in the interval $\Delta_2 = [-1,1]$. The uncertainty domain is $\Delta = \Delta_1 \times \Delta_2$. The nominal parameter vector is $\bar{q} = (0,0)$; a parameter vector instance is $q_a = (-1,-1)$.

2.2   LPGUM Coordinate

A *Linear Parametric Geometric Uncertainty Model (LPGUM)* coordinate $d(q)$ is an uncertain coordinate defined by a nominal value $\bar{d}$ and a k-dimensional column *sensitivity vector* A_d over a parametric uncertainty model $(q, \bar{q}, \Delta)$. Entry $(A_d)_j$ is a constant that quantifies the sensitivity of the coordinate to parameter q_j; it is zero, when the coordinate is independent of q_j. The LPGUM of $d(q)$ is:

$$d(q) = \bar{d} + qA_d$$

The *uncertainty zone of coordinate* $d(q)$ is the set of all coordinate values for instances of parameter vector q:

$$Z(d(q)) = \{d \mid d = \bar{d} + qA_d, q \in \Delta\}$$

The uncertainty zone of a coordinate is the real-valued interval $[\min d(q), \max d(q)], q \in \Delta$. For example, in Fig. 2.1(a), the nominal value of the x coordinate of LPGUM point is 0 and its sensitivity vector A_d is $(1, 6)$; its uncertainty zone is the interval $[-8, 8]$.

Two coordinates defined over the same parametric model are said to be *dependent* iff they both depend on at least one common parameter. Otherwise, they are *independent*.

For example, in Fig. 2.1(a), the nominal value of the x and y coordinates of LPGUM point $s(q)$ is 0 and their sensitivity vectors are $(1, 6)$ and $(-1, 3)$, respectively. Thus, the coordinates are dependent since they both depend on parameters q_1 and q_2.

2.3   LPGUM Point and Vector

An *LPGUM point* $s(q)$ in the plane is an uncertain point defined by the *nominal point* $\bar{s} = (\bar{d}_x, \bar{d}_y)$, where $\bar{d}_x, \bar{d}_y$ are the nominal x and y point coordinates, and A_s is a $k \times 2$ sensitivity matrix over a parametric uncertainty model $(q, \bar{q}, \Delta)$. The uncertain location of the point is $s(q) = (d_x(q), d_y(q))$, where $d_x(q)$ and $d_y(q)$ are LPGUM coordinates. Entries $(A_s)_{j,x}, (A_s)_{j,y}$ of matrix A_s are constants that quantify the sensitivity of the point's coordinates to parameter q_j. Entry $(A_s)_{j,x} = 0$ when coordinate x is independent of q_j; entry $(A_s)_{j,y} = 0$ when coordinate y is independent of q_j. When the entire row $(A_s)_{j,*} = 0$, the point location is independent of q_j. The LPGUM of $s(q)$ is:

$$s(q) = \bar{s} + qA_s$$

An instance of $s(q)$ is a point $s(q_a) = \bar{s} + q_a A_s$ for a given parameter instance $q_a \in \Delta$. The *uncertainty zone of a point* is defined as the set of all point locations for all parameter instances q:

$$Z(s(q)) = \{s | s = \bar{s} + q A_s, q \in \Delta\}$$

We denote the envelope of the uncertainty zone $Z(s(q))$ by $\partial Z(s(q))$. The uncertainty zone of a point $Z(s(q))$ is bounded by a zonotope — a centrally symmetric convex polygon with at most $2k$ vertices and edges. The zonotope of LPGUM point $s(q)$ is defined by its vertices in counterclockwise order $S = \langle p_1, p_2, \ldots, p_k \rangle$ with at most $K \leq 2k$ vertices (Fig. 2.2(a)).

For example, in Fig. 2.1(a), the point is defined by nominal point $\bar{s} = (0,0)$; its sensitivity matrix is $A_s = \begin{pmatrix} 1 & -1 \\ 6 & 3 \end{pmatrix}$. For parameter instance $q_a = (-1,-1)$, the point instance is $s(q_a) = (0,0) + (-1,-1)\begin{pmatrix} 1 & -1 \\ 6 & 3 \end{pmatrix} = (-7,-2)$. The zonotope is defined by four vertices: $S = \langle (8,1), (4,5), (-8,-1), (-4,-5) \rangle$.

An *LPGUM vector* $\vec{v}(q) = (d_x(q), d_y(q))$ is an uncertain vector defined by its origin $(0,0)$ and an LPGUM point $v(q) = (d_x(q), d_y(q))$ as above. The nominal direction of $\vec{v}(q)$ is denoted by $\vec{v}$.

For example, in Fig 2.1(a), a vector is defined by nominal direction $\vec{v} = (4,4)$; its sensitivity matrix is $A_s = \begin{pmatrix} 1 & -1 \\ 0 & 0 \end{pmatrix}$. For parameter

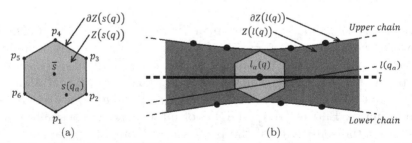

(a)   (b)

Fig. 2.2.   Illustration of LPGUM point and line: (a) LPGUM point $s(q)$ and its uncertainty zone $Z(s(q))$ (light gray). The nominal point location is $\bar{s}$; $s(q_a)$ is a point instance for the parameter vector instance q_a. The uncertainty zone envelope $\partial Z(s(q))$ is a zonotope defined by the point list $\langle p_1, p_2, \ldots, p_6 \rangle$; (b) LPGUM line $l(q)$ and its the uncertainty zone $Z(l(q))$ (dark gray). The nominal line location is $\bar{l}$; $l(q_a)$ is a line instance for the parameter vector instance q_a. The uncertainty zone envelope $\partial Z(l(q))$ is defined by two segment chains, where each chain is a list of consecutive line and parabola segments with shared endpoints (in black points). A value of α yields an LPGUM point $l_\alpha(q)$ (in light gray).

instance $q_a = (-1, -1)$, the vector instance is $\vec{v}(q_a) = (4, 4) +$ $(-1, -1)\begin{pmatrix} 1 & -1 \\ 0 & 0 \end{pmatrix} = (3, 5)$.

An *LPGUM point set* $S(q)$ in the plane is a set of n LPGUM points $S(q) = \{s_1(q), s_2(q), \ldots, s_n(q)\}$ defined by *nominal point set* $\overline{S} = \{\overline{s}_1, \overline{s}_2, \ldots, \overline{s}_n\}$ and by n $k \times 2$ *sensitivity matrices* $A_1, A_2, \ldots, A_n$ over the *same* parametric uncertainty model $(q, \overline{q}, \Delta)$. The uncertain location of a point is $s_i(q) = (d_{ix}, (q), d_{iy}(q))$ where $d_{ix}(q)$ and $d_{iy}(q)$ are LPGUM coordinates; the nominal location of a point is $\overline{s}_i = (\overline{d}_{ix}\overline{d}_{iy})$. The uncertainty zone is the zonotope $Z(s_i(q))$ and its envelope is $\partial Z(s_i(q))$. The zonotope $Z(s_i(q))$ is defined by its vertices in counterclockwise order: $S_i = \langle p_{i1}, p_{i2}, \ldots, p_{iK} \rangle$.

The dependencies between the point uncertainties are described by n $k \times 2$ sensitivity matrices $A_1, A_2, \ldots, A_n$ that state the dependence of the point locations on the parameter vector q. Entries $(A_i)_{j,x}, (A_i)_{j,y}, 1 \leq i \leq n, 1 \leq j \leq k$ are constants that quantify the sensitivity of coordinates x and y of point $s_i(q) = (d_{ix}(q), d_{iy}(q))$, respectively, to parameter q_j. When $d_{ix}(q)$ is independent of q_j, entry $(A_i)_{j,x} = 0$; when $d_{iy}(q)$ is independent of q_j, entry $(A_i)_{j,y} = 0$; when the entire row $(A_i)_{j,*} = 0$, point $s_i(q)$ is independent of q_j. When the entire rows $(A_i)_{j,*} = 0$ for all points, the uncertainty of the point set $S(q)$ is independent of q_j.

A set of LPGUM points is said to be *dependent* iff at least two coordinates of two or more LPGUM points depend on at least one common parameter. Otherwise, the LPGUM point set is *independent*.

The LPGUM point set $S(q)$ is a family of point sets for every given parameter instance $q_a \in \Delta$: The set $S(q_a)$ is the set of points $s_i(q_a)$ for instance $q_a \in \Delta$ of the parameter vector q. In the following, we assume that no two point zonotopes $Z(s_i(q)), Z(s_j(q)), 1 \leq i \neq j \leq n$, intersect. This can be detected in $O(n \log n + m)$ time, where m is the number of intersecting pairs [58].

2.4 LPGUM Line and Edge

An *LPGUM line* $l(q)$ in the plane is an uncertain line defined by *nominal line* $\overline{l}$ and two $k \times 2$ sensitivity matrices A_u, A_v over a parametric uncertainty model $(q, \overline{q}, \Delta)$. The uncertain location of the line is $l(q) = u(q) + \alpha(\vec{v}(q)), \alpha \in \mathbb{R}$, where $u(q)$ is an LPGUM point and

$\vec{v}(q)$ is an LPGUM vector. The nominal line is $\bar{l} = \bar{u} + \alpha\vec{v}, \alpha \in \mathbb{R}$. Entries $(A_u)_{j,x}, (A_u)_{j,y}$ of matrix A_u are constants that quantify the sensitivity of coordinate x, y of LPGUM point $u(q)$ to parameter q_j. Entry $(A_u)_{j,x} = 0$ when coordinate x of point $u(q)$ is independent of q_j; entry $(A_u)_{j,y} = 0$ when coordinate y of point $u(q)$ is independent of q_j. When the entire row $(A_u)_{j,*} = 0$, the point $u(q)$ is independent of q_j. Matrix A_v is defined similarly. When the entire rows $(A_u)_{j,*}(A_v)_{j,*} = 0$, the LPGUM line $l(q)$ is independent of parameter q_j. An instance of line $l(q)$ is $l(q_a) = u(q_a) + \alpha(\vec{v}(q_a))$ for vector $q_a \in \Delta$. We denote the line envelope of the uncertainty zone $Z(l(q))$ by $\partial Z(l(q))$.

For example, in Fig. 2.1(b), the line is defined by the point $s(q) = (0,0) + q\begin{pmatrix} 1 & -1 \\ 6 & 3 \end{pmatrix}$ and the vector $\vec{v}(q) = (4,4) + q\begin{pmatrix} 1 & -1 \\ 0 & 0 \end{pmatrix}$; the nominal line is $\bar{l} = (0,0) + \alpha(4,4)$. For parameter instance $q_a = (-1,-1)$, the line instance is $l(q_a) = (0,0) + (-1,-1)\begin{pmatrix} 1 & -1 \\ 6 & 3 \end{pmatrix} +$

$\alpha((4,4) + (-1,-1)\begin{pmatrix} 1 & -1 \\ 0 & 0 \end{pmatrix}) = (-7,-2) + \alpha(3,5).$

An *LPGUM edge* is defined as an LPGUM line with $\alpha \in [1,0]$.

The line envelope consists of two monotone *segment chains* with $O(k)$ segments each (Fig. 2.2(b)). A segment chain is a list of consecutive line and parabola segments with shared endpoints. The segment chain is monotonic with respect to nominal line $\bar{l}$. Every value of α yields an LPGUM point $l_\alpha(q)$.

For example, in Fig. 2.1(b), the line envelope consists of two monotone segment chains with two segments each (black continuous lines); for $\alpha = 0$, the point is $l_0(q) = (0,0) + q\begin{pmatrix} 1 & -1 \\ 6 & 3 \end{pmatrix}$.

Note that an LPGUM line may not have an envelope. This occurs when the origin is inside the uncertainty zone of the LPGUM vector that defines the LPGUM line. In this case, a line instance can be oriented in any direction, so the line uncertainty zone spans the entire plane and the LPGUM line does not have an envelope. This can be detected by computing the uncertainty zone of the LPGUM vector in $O(k \log k)$ time and testing if the origin is inside it in $O(k)$ time. In the following, we will assume that an LPGUM line has an envelope.

2.5 LPGUM Three-Point Circle

An *LPGUM three-point circle* $c_{uvw}(q)$ is an uncertain circle defined by *nominal three-point circle* $\bar{c}_{uvw}$ and three $k \times 2$ sensitivity matrices $A_u, A_v A_w$ over the **same** parametric uncertainty model $(q, \bar{q}, \Delta)$. The uncertain location of the three-point circle is $c_{uvw}(q) = circle(u(q), v(q), w(q))$ where $u(q), v(q)$ and $w(q)$ are LPGUM points; the nominal location of three-point circle is $\bar{c}_{uvw} = circle(\bar{u}, \bar{v}, \bar{w})$ (Fig. 2.3). The LPGUM three-point circle is

$$c_{uvw}(q) = \text{circle}(u(q), v(q), w(q))$$
$$= \text{circle}(\bar{u} + qA_u, \bar{v} + qA_v, \bar{w} + qA_w)$$

An instance of $c_{uvw}(q)$ is circle $c_{uvw}(q_a) = \text{circle}(u(q_a), v(q_a), w(q_a))$ for parameter vector $q_a \in \Delta$ (Fig. 2.3). An LPGUM three-point circle is said to be *dependent* iff at least two coordinates or more of its defining LPGUM points depend on at least one common parameter; otherwise, it is *independent*.

The *uncertainty zone of a three-point circle* is defined by the set difference of the union and intersection of all three-point circle

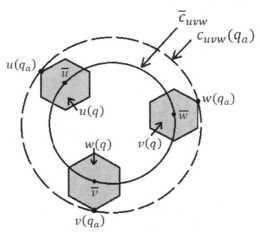

Fig. 2.3. An LPGUM three-point circle $c_{uvw}(q)$. The nominal three-point circle location is $\bar{c}_{uvw}$ (solid black circle) and is defined by the nominal points $\bar{u}, \bar{v}, \bar{w}$ (black dots); $c_{uve}(q_a)$ is a circle instance for the parameter vector instance q_a (dashed circle) defined by point instances $u(q_a), v(q_a), w(q_a)$.

instances:

$$Z(c_{uvw}(q)) = CU_{uvw} - CI_{uvw}$$

$$CU_{uvw} = \bigcup_{q \in \Delta} \text{circle}(u(q), v(q), w(q))$$

$$CI_{uvw} = \bigcap_{q \in \Delta} \text{circle}(u(q), v(q), w(q))$$

where the union is CU_{uvw} and the intersection is CI_{uvw} of all three-point circle instances (Fig. 2.4). We denote by ∂CU_{uvw} and by ∂CI_{uvw} the outer and inner envelopes of $Z(c_{uvw}(q))$, respectively.

Let p be a point in the plane. Then, $\forall p \in CU_{uvw}, \exists q_a \in \Delta$ so that p is inside the three-point circle $c_{uvw}(q_a)$. Similarly, $\forall p \notin CU_{uvw}$, p is outside three-point circle $c_{uvw}(q_a), \forall q_a \in \Delta$. And, $\forall p \in CI_{uvw}$, p is inside three-point circle $c_{uvw}(q_a), \forall q_a \in \Delta$. And, $\forall p \in Z(c_{uvw}(q)), \exists q_a q_b \in \Delta$ for which p is inside three-point circle $c_{uvw}(q_a)$ and p is outside three-point circle $c_{uvw}(q_b)$ (Fig. 2.4(c)).

The envelope of the uncertainty zone $Z(c_{uvw}(q))$ consists of an outer envelope ∂CU_{uvw} and an inner envelope ∂CI_{uvw} (Fig. 2.4(a and b)). Both envelopes are formed by arc segments of a three-point circle instance $c_{uvw}(q_a)$, denoted by $outer\_arc(c_{uvw}(q_a))$ and $inner\_arc(c_{uvw}(q_a))$ (Fig. 2.4(c)).

Note that an LPGUM three-point circle may not have an envelope. This occurs when three-point instances are collinear (Fig. 2.5).

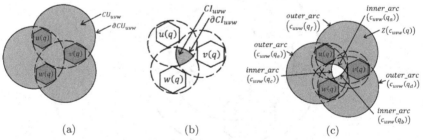

(a)   (b)   (c)

Fig. 2.4.   Illustration of the outer and inner envelopes and uncertainty zone of an LPGUM three-point circle defined by LPGUM points $u(q), v(q), w(q)$: (a) outer envelope ∂CU_{uvw} (solid arcs) is defined by the three-point circle union CU_{uvw} (gray region); (b) inner envelope ∂CI_{uvw} (solid arcs) is defined by the three-point circle intersection CI_{uvw} (gray region); (c) uncertainty zone $Z(c_{uvw}(q))$ (in gray); its outer envelope consists of three arc segments: $outer\_arc(c_{uvw}(q_d))$, $outer\_arc(c_{uvw}(q_e))$, $outer\_arc(c_{uvw}(q_f))$; its inner envelope consists of three arc segments: $inner\_arc(c_{uvw}(q_a))$, $inner\_arc(c_{uvw}(q_b))$, $inner\_arc(c_{uvw}(q_c))$.

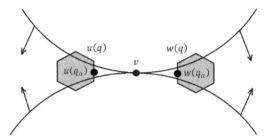

Fig. 2.5. Illustration of two LPGUM points $u(q), w(q)$ (in gray) and an exact point v such that the three points $u(q_a), v, w(q_a)$ (black dots) that define the three-point circle are collinear. In this case, the circle uncertainty zone CU_{uvw} spans the entire plane.

This situation can be detected by the algorithms described in Section 3.3.1 in $O(k)$ time for the independent case and $O(k^2)$ time for the dependent case. In the following, we will assume that an LPGUM three-point circle has an envelope.

2.6 Summary

This chapter described the LPGUM. LPGUM allows the systematic study of basic geometric entities and their relations. In LPGUM, basic geometric features, such as coordinates, points, vectors, lines, edges and circles, are defined by a common set of parameters with uncertainty intervals. The uncertainty zones around nominal feature locations are defined by uncertainty sensitivity matrices whose entries indicate the coordinates' sensitivity to parameter variations and their dependencies. The sensitivity matrices allow modeling of the full range of uncertainty dependency and parameter coupling, from independence through partial dependency, to complete dependency. LPGUM allows for describing and efficient handling of geometric objects with dependent uncertainty.

Chapter 3

The Envelopes of Uncertain Points, Lines and Circles

This chapter describes algorithms for computing the uncertainty envelopes of elementary geometric entities: coordinates, points, lines and circles. Section 3.1 presents methods for computing the envelope of the LPGUM coordinate and point. Section 3.2 describes the properties of the envelope of the an LPGUM line and presents a new algorithm for computing it. Section 3.3 presents the properties of the envelope of the LPGUM three-point circle and an efficient algorithm for computing it. Section 3.4 summarizes this chapter.

3.1 LPGUM Coordinate and Point

The uncertainty zone of a coordinate is the interval $[\min d(q), \max d(q)]$. It is directly computed in optimal $\theta(k)$ time.

The uncertainty zone of a point is bounded by a zonotope — a centrally symmetric convex polygon with at most $2k$ vertices and edges (Section 2.3). The zonotope is the feasible region of the linear programming problem:

$$\max_{q \in \Delta} \langle A_s d, q \rangle \tag{3.1}$$

where $\langle , \rangle$ is the vector inner product. The maximal displacement of $s(q)$ in direction d occurs at extremal parameter values q_j^-, q_j^+:

$$p_d = \bar{s} + \sum_{i=1}^{K} q_i^d (A_s)_{i,*} \tag{3.2}$$

where the sign of each parameter q_i is determined by

$$q_i^d = \begin{cases} q_i^+ & \text{for } \langle (A_s)_{i,*}, d \rangle > 0 \\ q_i^- & \text{for } \langle (A_s)_{i,*}, d \rangle < 0 \\ 0 & \text{for } \langle (A_s)_{i,*}, d \rangle = 0 \end{cases}$$

The corresponding sign vector is the k-dimensional vector in which "+" stands for q_i^+ and "−" stands for q_i^-.

The vertices of the point uncertainty envelope are computed as follows. Each sensitivity matrix row $(A_s)_{i,*}$ is interpreted as a vector that induces a line L_i perpendicular to it, passing through the origin. The lines L_i, $i \in 1, \ldots, K$ induce a planar subdivision, called the **cone diagram**, whose cells are cones, bound by the two lines defined by their corresponding column vectors (Fig. 3.1). We sort the lines, L_i, in increasing angle order and visit the cones in counterclockwise order. We compute the sign vector of the first cone (Eq. (3.2)), move to its neighbor and update its corresponding sign vector, by finding the parameter value q_i that changes — from q_i^+ to q_i^-, or vice versa.

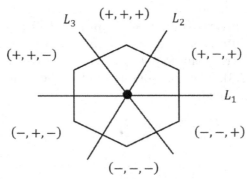

Fig. 3.1.   Illustration of the cone diagram induced by the three lines L_1, L_2, L_3 and their corresponding sign vectors (+ indicates left of the line, − indicates right of the line).

The corresponding point uncertainty envelope vertex is then computed using Eq. (3.2). Iterating over all cones yields the zonotope vertices. This algorithm yields the following theorem which was first proven in Ref. [50].

Theorem 3.1. *The uncertainty zone boundary of an LPGUM point, defined over a parametric uncertainty model, is a zonotope with, at most, $2k < K$ vertices, computed in optimal $\theta(k \log k)$ time and $O(k)$ space, where k is the number of parameters in q.*

3.2 LPGUM Line

We now describe an efficient algorithm for computing the envelope of an LPGUM line in $O(k^2)$ time. This algorithm improves the $O(k^2 \log k)$ time algorithm described in Ref. [54]. Section 3.2.1 presents the definition and properties of the LPGUM line. Section 3.2.2 describes the cone diagram mapping. Section 3.2.3 describes the algorithm.

3.2.1 Definitions and properties

Let $l(q) = u(q) + \alpha(\vec{v}(q)) = \bar{u} + qA_u + \alpha(\vec{v} + qA_v), \alpha \in \mathbb{R}$, be an LPGUM line. Let $A_\alpha = A_u + \alpha A_v$. Each sensitivity matrix row $(A_\alpha)_{i,*} = (A_u)_{i,*} + \alpha(A_v)_{i,*}$ of the point $l_\alpha(q)$ is a vector $\vec{d_i}$ that induces a line L_i perpendicular to it and passing through the origin. The lines $L_i, i \in \{1, \ldots, k\}$ induce a planar subdivision, called **cone diagram**, whose cells are open cones bound by two lines (Fig. 3.1).

When the vectors corresponding to $(A_u)_{i,*}$ and $(A_v)_{i,*}$ are not collinear, then, as α approaches $-\infty$, $(A_\alpha)_{i,*}$ approaches a vector in the direction of $-(A_v)_{i,*}$. When $\alpha = 0$, $(A_\alpha)_{i,*} = (A_u)_{i,*}$ and as α approaches ∞, $(A_\alpha)_{i,*}$ approaches a vector in the direction of $(A_v)_{i,*}$. The transition from the direction of $-(A_v)_{i,*}$ through $(A_u)_{i,*}$ to the direction of $(A_v)_{i,*}$ is continuous and in a constant direction. We call such a rotation **monotonic**. Thus, $(A_\alpha)_{i,*}$ is monotonic in a range of π radians. Consequently, the corresponding line in the cone diagram of $l_\alpha(q)$ also rotates monotonically in a range of π radians. Note that every line of the cone diagram may rotate at a different speed and direction, depending on the relative size and direction of the vectors $(A_u)_{i,*}$ and $(A_v)_{i,*}$.

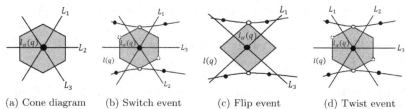

(a) Cone diagram   (b) Switch event   (c) Flip event   (d) Twist event

Fig. 3.2. Illustration of the cone diagram and the cone diagram events defined by point $l_\alpha(q)$ defined by three parameters. The supporting vertices of $l_\alpha(q)$ are shown as white dots, while the shared line and parabola segment chains of line $l(q)$ are shown as black dots: (a) lines L_1, L_2, L_3 of the cone diagram; (b) switch event between lines L_2 and L_3 — the supporting vertices before the event are shown as dotted white points; (c) flip event of line L_2 — the event does not involve the supporting vertices so it does not affect the line envelope; (d) twist event — a different part of $l_\alpha(q)$ is in contact with the envelope; the supporting vertices before the event are shown as dotted white points.

For example, in Fig. 2.1(b), the vectors corresponding to $(A_s)_{1,*} = (1,-1)$ and $(A_v)_{1,*} = (1,-1)$ are collinear, so as α approaches $-\infty$, $(A_\alpha)_{1,*}$ approaches a vector in the direction of $-(A_v)_{1,*}$, which is the same direction of $-(A_s)_{1,*}$. For $\alpha = -1$, $(A_\alpha)_{1,*}$ the vector vanishes and as α approaches ∞, $(A_\alpha)_{1,*}$ approaches a vector in the direction of $(A_v)_{1,*}$, the same direction of $(A_s)_{1,*}$; so, the direction of $(A_\alpha)_{1,*}$ is constant and is same as that of $(A_v)_{1,*}$.

As α varies from $-\infty$ to $+\infty$, three types of events can occur: **switch events**, **flip events** and **twist events** (Fig. 3.2). Switch events and flip events are called topological events, as they affect the topology of the cone diagram of $l_\alpha(q)$. Twist events are non-topological events.

A **switch event** (Fig. 3.2(b)) occurs at a value of α for which two lines of the cone diagram of the point $l_\alpha(q)$ coincide. These are values of α such that $\langle (A_\alpha)_{i,*}, (A_\alpha)_{j,*}^{\perp} \rangle = 0$. Switch events occur only between neighboring lines. For example, in Fig. 2.1(b), there are no switch events.

A **flip event** (Fig. 3.2(c)) occurs at a value of α for which a row vector $(A_\alpha)_{i,*}$ equals zero. These are values of α such that $(A_\alpha)_{i,*} = 0$. When the vectors $(A_u)_{i,*}$ and $(A_v)_{i,*}$ are collinear, there exists a value of α for which $(A_\alpha)_{i,*}$ vanishes. For example, in Fig. 2.1(b), a flip event occurs at $\alpha = -1$, where $(A_\alpha)_{1,*} = 0$.

A **twist event** (Fig. 3.2(d)) occurs when $l_\alpha(q)$, or part of it, rotates so that a different part of it is in contact with the line's envelope. This occurs when two or more lines of the cone diagram rotate in the same direction, and so part (or all) of the zonotope rotates as well. These are values of α for which $l(q^{(i)}) = l(q^{(j)})$, where $q^{(i)}$ and $q^{(j)}$ are parameterizations of neighboring vertices on the zonotope of $l_\alpha(q)$. For example, in Fig. 2.1(b), there are no twist events.

Lemma 3.1. *Let $l(q) = u(q) + \alpha(\vec{v}(q))$ be an LPGUM line. Every vertex on the uncertainty envelope of $l(q)$ is the result of an event.*

Proof. As α changes, the LPGUM point $l_\alpha(q)$ moves, tracing out the uncertainty envelope. When there are no topological events, the vertices of $l_\alpha(q)$ each follow a line instance.

An event is said to be **relevant** if it affects the envelope of the line, that is, it involves the line of the cone diagram which defines the supporting vertices or the endpoints of the supporting segments. Consider a relevant topological event. At the value of α at which the event occurs, the vertex changes direction by moving to another line instance, thereby creating a vertex on the uncertainty envelope. When there are no topological events, a change in the envelope of the line occurs, only if the line instances being followed by the vertices cross each other. This is the definition of a twist event. Thus, every vertex on the uncertainty envelope is a result of a topological event or a twist event. □

For every value of α, there is a part of the zonotope that is tangential to the envelope. When the zonotope is tangential to the envelope at a vertex, the vertex is called a **supporting vertex**. When the zonotope is tangential to the envelope along a segment, it is called a **supporting segment**. For example, in Fig. 2.1(b), the zonotopes are tangential to the envelope vertices.

Since there are $O(k^2)$ topological events, at most $2k$ relevant topological events and at most $O(k)$ twist events that affect the line's uncertainty zone. We prove this next with the following two Lemmas and a Theorem.

Lemma 3.2. *Let $l(q)$ be an LPGUM line. The two connected components outside the uncertainty zone of $l(q)$ are both convex.*

Proof. The interior of the uncertainty zone of the line is the union of all instances of $l(q)$. Thus, through every point in the uncertainty

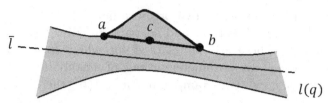

Fig. 3.3.   Illustration of two points a, b on the boundary of the uncertainty zone of $l(q)$ that form a Jordan curve; point c is on the segment ab.

zone, there is at least one straight line, completely contained in the uncertainty zone.

Assume by contradiction that one of the regions to one side of the uncertainty zone is not convex (Fig. 3.3). Let a and b be two points in this non-convex region, outside the uncertainty zone. Thus, it is possible to choose points a and b so that the segment connecting them is not completely contained in the region in question. Let c be one of the points on the segment ab that is in the uncertainty zone. Note that the segment ab and part of the uncertainty envelope create a Jordan curve. Thus, any straight line going through c must intersect the uncertainty envelope — a contradiction.   □

Lemma 3.3. *Let $l(q)$ be an LPGUM line. The region to one side of the uncertainty zone of $l(q)$ is unbounded.*

Proof.   Let $l(q_e)$ be line instance and let $l_{\alpha 1}(q_e), l_{\alpha 2}(q_e), \ldots, l_{\alpha n}(q_e)$ be points on $l(q_e)$ ordered in increasing value of α. Note that this is the order of the points on the line and that this order is preserved for all instances of the line. We call this the ***stabbing order*** of the line.

Suppose by contradiction that the region is bounded. By Lemma 3.2, this region must be convex. Let (α, β) and (γ, δ) be two pairs of antipodal vertices on its boundary. Let $l_{\alpha}(q), l_{\beta}(q), l_{\gamma}(q)$ and $l_{\delta}(q)$ be four distinct LPGUM points on the line, incident on α, β, γ and δ, respectively. Let $q_a, q_b \in \Delta$ be two instances of parameter vectors, so that $l(q_a)$ and $l(q_b)$ are line instances going through α and β, respectively. Due to the convexity of the zonotopes and of the area in question, the stabbing order of the two lines $l(q_a)$ and $l(q_b)$ with respect to the points $l_{\alpha}(q), l_{\beta}(q), l_{\gamma}(q)$ and $l_{\delta}(q)$ cannot be the same. This contradicts the fact that all the line instances must have the same stabbing order.   □

Theorem 3.2. *Let U be one of the two boundaries of the uncertainty zone of line l(q). Then there exists a nominal line with respect to which U is monotonic.*

Proof.   The theorem follows from Lemmas 3.2 and 3.3.   □

Lemma 3.4. *Let $l(q)$ be an LPGUM line defined over a parametric uncertainty model. There are at most $2k$ relevant topological events.*

Proof.   To find all the flip events, the equation $(A_\alpha)_{i,*} = 0$ is solved for every $i = 1, \ldots, k$. There are k linear equations; thus, there cannot be more than k flip events.

To bound the number of relevant switch events, we show that every line in the cone diagram of $l_\alpha(q)$ can take part in one switch event. We show this by considering every possible outcome of a relevant switch event and showing that once a line of the cone diagram has participated in a relevant switch event, it cannot participate in another one. For every value of α, there is a part of the zonotope tangential to the envelope. If a supporting vertex (or at least one end of a supporting segment) is to one side of a line of the cone diagram before a switch event, and after the event the supporting vertex (or both ends of a supporting segment) is on the other side of the line, it is said that the line went through the envelope direction.

By Theorem 3.2, we assume, without loss of generality, that the upper envelope is x monotone, and that, with increasing values of α, $l_\alpha(q)$ moves to the right. As the value of α increases, the slope of the upper envelope increases. This means that a line tangential to the upper envelope turns counterclockwise, as the value of α increases. Thus, the upper envelope turns counterclockwise.

We prove next that, at every relevant switch event, at least one line of the cone diagram passes through the direction of the envelope. Let L_e, L_f, L_g and L_h be four lines of the cone diagram of $l_\alpha(q)$ (Fig. 3.4). Let there be a switch event involving L_f and L_g at α_0, and let the lines be ordered (Fig. 3.4(a)) right before the event (Fig. 3.4(b)) and right after it. To account for all possible outcomes of switch events, we must consider all possible settings right before the events and for each we must allow for every outcome. The possible cases are as follows:

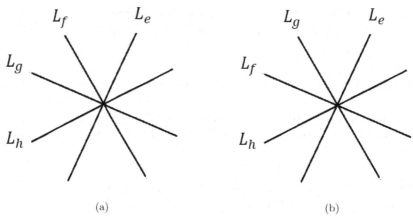

(a)   (b)

Fig. 3.4.   The cone diagram of four lines L_h, L_g, L_f, L_e: (a) before and (b) after a switch event of L_g and L_f.

Case 1 (vertex–vertex): Right before the event, the envelope is supported by a vertex and after the event it is also supported by a vertex.

Case 2 (segment–vertex): Right before the event, the envelope is supported by a segment and after the event it is supported by a vertex.

Case 3 (vertex–segment): Right before the event, the envelope is supported by a vertex and after the event it is supported by a segment.

Case 4 (segment–segment): Right before the event, the envelope is supported by a segment and after the event it is also supported by a segment.

We consider each of the four cases in detail next.

Case 1: Suppose that, right before the event, the envelope is supported by a vertex that corresponds to the cone $L_f L_g$ or a segment, such that one of its endpoints corresponds to that cone. If, before the event, the envelope is supported by a vertex, and it is also supported by a vertex after the event, then the supporting vertex after the event must correspond to one of the cones $L_e L_g$, $L_g L_f$ or $L_f L_h$. In all three cases, at least one of the lines L_f or L_g has gone through the direction of the envelope.

Cases 2 and 3: Suppose that before the event, the envelope is supported by a segment that has one end associated with the cone $L_f L_g$ and the other associated with the cone $L_e L_f$ and after the event it is supported by a vertex in $L_e L_g$, then L_f has gone through the direction of the envelope. Symmetrically, if, before the event, the envelope is supported by a segment associated with the cones $L_f L_g$ and $L_g L_h$, and after the event, it is supported by a vertex associated with $L_f L_h$, then the line L_g has gone through the direction of the envelope. In both cases, if, after the event, the envelope is supported by a vertex associated with $L_g L_f$, then one of the lines L_g or L_f has gone through the direction of the envelope. This covers Case 2 (segment-vertex) and Case 3 (vertex-segment) with the values of α decreasing (increasing) starting with the envelope supported by a segment (vertex) and ending with the envelope supported by a segment.

Case 4: The envelope is supported by a segment both before and after the event. If, before the event, the segment is associated with the cones $L_e L_f$ and $L_f L_g$, and after the event, with the cones $L_e L_g$ and $L_e L_f$, then L_f has gone through the direction of the envelope. Symmetrically, if, before the event, the segment is associated with the cones $L_f L_g$ and $L_g L_h$, and after the event with the cones $L_g L_f$ and $L_f L_h$, then L_g has gone through the direction of the envelope. If, before the event, the segment is associated with the cones $L_e L_f$ and $L_f L_g$, and after the event, with the cones $L_g L_f$ and $L_f L_h$, then L_g has gone through the direction of the envelope. Symmetrically, if, before the event, the segment is associated with the cones $L_f L_g$ and $L_g L_h$, and after the event, with the cones $L_e L_g$ and $L_g L_f$, then L_f has gone through the direction of the envelope. As these are all the possible changes that can take place at a switch event, we conclude that, at every switch event, at least one line of the cone diagram goes through the direction of the envelope.

Let L be the line of the cone diagram that passes through the direction of the envelope. When L rotates clockwise, it will not meet the envelope again. This is because the lines of the cone diagram rotate monotonically clockwise or counterclockwise, in a range of π radians, and, as a consequence of Lemmas 3.2–3.4, the envelope rotates monotonically in a range smaller than π radians.

We now prove by contradiction that when L rotates in the same direction as the envelope, it can go through the direction of the envelope only once. We assume, without loss of generality that L rotates counterclockwise, as the value of α increases, and that, as L goes through the direction of the envelope, the envelope moves to the negative side of L. Assume now by contradiction that there is another relevant switch event, at which L goes through the direction of the envelope. This might happen for one of two reasons. The first is that the entire LPGUM point rotated significantly, so L could meet the envelope again while rotating. But, this cannot happen, as the rotation of the LPGUM point would involve L rotating clockwise, contrary to the assumption. The second possibility is that some topological event, not involving L, pushes the envelope back, into the positive half-plane of L. This cannot happen, as topological events not involving L would not affect the sign of the parameter associated with L, so the envelope cannot be on the positive side of L.

At every relevant switch event, at least one line of the cone diagram goes through the direction of the envelope, and every line of the cone diagram can go through the direction of the envelope only once (if at all). Thus, there are not more than k relevant switch events.   □

We use a sweep line technique to compute the line envelope by sequentially processing each one of the events as follows. We sweep the values of α from a small value before any event to a large value after the last event. As the values of α change, the zonotope $l_\alpha(q)$ slides along the line, tracing out the line's envelope (Fig. 2.1(b)). Every vertex of $l_\alpha(q)$ follows a line instance defined by the value of q at the vertex. The sweep stops at events. The algorithm iterates over all the events, tracing out the uncertainty envelope segments and finding new events. When the event queue is empty, the segments are combined. At topological events, the cone diagram changes, so the vertices of $l_\alpha(q)$ start a new line instance. At twist events, the line instances being followed by vertices of $l_\alpha(q)$ intersect each other.

To find an initial value for α, we compute all flip events and add them to the event queue. We set α to a value smaller than the smallest value found. We then compute switch events among all neighboring lines, and set α to a value smaller than the smallest value found. This is repeated until there is no need to change the value of α. The same procedure is now followed for twist events. Finding the initial value will take a time of $O(k^2)$, as there are no more than k flip events and k^2 switch events and, in the absence of topological events, there are no more than k twist events.

Each type of event is handled differently. For flip events, the value of the parameter corresponding to the flipped line in the cone diagram is negated for all vertices of the point's envelope. For switch events, the values of the parameters corresponding to the lines involved are negated for the two vertices corresponding to the cones bounded by both of the lines, and new switch events are computed for the new neighboring lines in the cone diagram. For twist events, no updating action is necessary. For every type of event, we sweep the zonotope, from the previous value of α to the current one.

We collect the segments of the boundary of all the sweeps, in a set of segments. Switch events cause new lines of the cone diagram to become neighbors. Thus, we test for new events, and add them to the queue. Once the event has been handled, all parts of the envelope that are covered by the line, at values smaller than α, will have been added to the set of segments, and all new switch events will have been found. When the event queue is empty, we compute the line's envelope, by finding the upper and lower envelope of the segments in the set of segments.

3.2.2   Cone diagram mapping: Definition and properties

The cone diagrams of the points on line $l(q)$ are defined in Cartesian space. Next, we define a mapping of the cone diagrams to a new space, called the (α, θ) space, $(x, y) \mapsto (\alpha, \theta)$, where α defines the LPGUM line $l(q) = u(q) + \alpha(\vec{v}(q)), \alpha \in \mathbb{R}$ and θ is an angle.

Let L_i be a line in the cone diagram. Line L_i passes through the origin and is perpendicular to each sensitivity matrix row vector $(A_\alpha)_{i,*} = (A_u)_{i,*} + \alpha(A_v)_{i,*}, 1 \leq i \leq k$. Denote $(A_u)_{i,x} = a, (A_u)_{i,y} = b, (A_v)_{i,x} = c, (A_v)_{i,y} = d$, where a, b, c, d are constants. Thus, $(A_\alpha)_{i,*} = (a + \alpha c, b + \alpha d)$ and $L_i = (-b - \alpha d, a + \alpha c)$. The angle θ is between the L_i and the positive x-direction (Fig. 3.2(a)):

$$\tan \theta = \frac{a + \alpha c}{-b - \alpha d} \qquad -\frac{1}{2}\pi < \theta < \frac{1}{2}\pi$$

Line L_i moves monotonically in a constant direction in a range of π radians, i.e., either counterclockwise or clockwise, unless

$(a, b), (c, d)$ are linearly dependent and L_i does not move (Fig. 3.5). When $-b - \alpha d = 0$, $\tan \theta$ is not defined and θ is set to $\frac{1}{2}\pi$ and $-\frac{1}{2}\pi$ radians as follows. When L_i passes through an angle of $\frac{1}{2}\pi$ radians in the counterclockwise direction, then in the (α, θ) space the corresponding line θ_i ends at $\frac{1}{2}\pi$ radians and continues with the same α value from $-\frac{1}{2}\pi$ radians (Fig. 3.2(a) and (b)). Similarly, when L_i passes through $-\frac{1}{2}\pi$ radians in the clockwise direction, then in the (α, θ) space the corresponding line θ_i ends at $-\frac{1}{2}\pi$ radians and continues with the same α value from $\frac{1}{2}\pi$ radians. Thus, line L_i in the cone diagram maps into curve $\theta_i(\alpha)$ and is defined by two curves θ_i^u and θ_i^d (Fig. 3.5). The two exceptions are as follows: (1) L_i moves from $-\frac{1}{2}\pi$ radians to $\frac{1}{2}\pi$ radians, in which case it defines a single curve; or (2) row vectors $(A_u)_{i,*}, (A_v)_{i,*}$ are linearly dependent and L_i does not move in which case it defines a vertical line.

By the definition of the curves $\theta_i^u, \theta_i^d, \theta_j^u, \theta_j^d$, only four types of intersections between them can occur: (1) intersection between θ_i^u

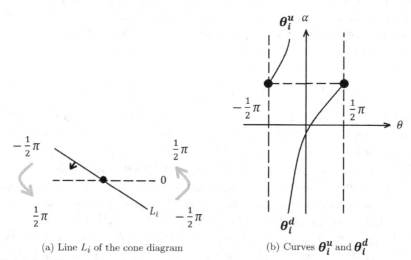

(a) Line L_i of the cone diagram   (b) Curves θ_i^u and θ_i^d

Fig. 3.5.   Illustration of the mapping of line L_i of the cone diagram from (x, y) space to (α, θ) space; (a) angle of line L_i of the cone diagram for point $l_\alpha(q)$ in (x, y) space when L_i rotates counterclockwise (black arrow) on the $-\frac{1}{2}\pi$ to $\frac{1}{2}\pi$ radians interval (light gray arrows); (b) graph of the function $\tan \theta = \frac{a + \dot{a}c}{-b - \alpha d}, -\frac{1}{2}\pi < \theta < \frac{1}{2}\pi$ where $a = 2, b = -2, c = 1, d = 2$. The corresponding curves in the (α, θ) space are θ_i^u and θ_i^d. Curve ends at $\frac{1}{2}\pi$ radians and continues with the same α value from $-\frac{1}{2}\pi$ radians.

and $\boldsymbol{\theta}_j^u$; (2) intersection between $\boldsymbol{\theta}_i^u$ and $\boldsymbol{\theta}_j^d$; (3) intersection between $\boldsymbol{\theta}_i^d$ and $\boldsymbol{\theta}_j^u$; (4) intersection between $\boldsymbol{\theta}_i^u$ and $\boldsymbol{\theta}_j^u$. Since every rotation of the line L_i in the cone diagram is monotonic in the π radians, the curves $\boldsymbol{\theta}_i^u, \boldsymbol{\theta}_i^d, \boldsymbol{\theta}_j^u, \boldsymbol{\theta}_j^d$ intersect at most once.

Lemma 3.5. *Curves* $\boldsymbol{\theta}_i^u, \boldsymbol{\theta}_i^d$ *and* $\boldsymbol{\theta}_j^u, \boldsymbol{\theta}_j^d$ *intersect in* (α, θ) *space at* α *iff a switch event between lines* L_i *and* L_j *occurs in* (x, y) *space for the same value of* α.

Proof. $\implies$ When curves $\boldsymbol{\theta}_i^u, \boldsymbol{\theta}_i^d$ and $\boldsymbol{\theta}_j^u, \boldsymbol{\theta}_j^d$ intersect for a value α, then L_i and L_j occur at the same angle in (x,y) space for this same value of α. This yields a switch event.

$\impliedby$ When a switch event between lines L_i and L_j occurs, then for some value of α, lines L_i and L_j are located at the same angle in (x, y) space. Thus, in (α, θ) space, $\boldsymbol{\theta}_i^u, \boldsymbol{\theta}_i^d$ and $\boldsymbol{\theta}_j^u, \boldsymbol{\theta}_j^d$ have the same value θ for this α, that is, $\boldsymbol{\theta}_i^u, \boldsymbol{\theta}_i^d$ and $\boldsymbol{\theta}_j^u, \boldsymbol{\theta}_j^d$ intersect. $\square$

As a consequence of Lemma 3.5, the switch event's order is preserved monotonically with respect to α.

3.2.3 LPGUM line envelope algorithm

The algorithm for computing the LPGUM line envelope in $O(k^2 \log k)$ was briefly described in Section 3.2.1. We describe next a more efficient $O(k^2)$ time algorithm that maps the lines of the cone diagram to curved lines of an arrangement. It extracts the $O(k)$ relevant switch events from it, instead of adding $O(k^2)$ switch events to the event queue, whose sorting requires $O(k^2 \log k)$ time. We first present two definitions and a Theorem from Ref. [59] and then describe the algorithm.

A *pseudoline* is a simple closed curve whose removal does not disconnect it.

An *arrangement of pseudolines* is a labeled set of pseudolines not all passing through the same point such that every pair intersects at most once.

Theorem 3.3. Zone theorem: *The sum of the numbers of sides in all the cells of an arrangement of* $n+1$ *pseudolines that are supported by one of the pseudolines is at most* $\frac{19n}{2} - 3$; *this bound is tight.*

Table 3.1.　Algorithm for computing the envelope of an LPGUM line.

Input: A LPGUM line $l(q) = v(q) + \alpha(\vec{v}(q))$, $\alpha \in \mathbb{R}$ and a parametric uncertainty model $(q, \bar{q}, \Delta)$.

1. Compute pseudoline arrangement $A(\hat{\theta})$;
2. Compute the initial value for α and insert all flip events in the event queue;
3. **While** *there is unhandled relevant event* **do**
   - a. Get the next flip event;
   - b. Compute the next relevant switch events by $A(\hat{\theta})$;
   - c. Compute the next relevant twist events;
   - d. **If** the event with the smallest value of α is not a flip event **then** set the flip event back to the queue;
   - e. Handle the event with the smallest value of α;
   - f. Add swept envelope segments to set of segments;
4. **End while**

Output: The envelope of line $l(q)$.

To find all the switch events for each line L_i in the cone diagram, we compute the curves $\boldsymbol{\theta}_i^u, \boldsymbol{\theta}_i^d$ in the (α, θ) space in $O(k)$ time. Then, we find the intersection between them (Section 3.1): each intersection is the solution of a quadratic equation which take a constant time. Overall, there are $O(k^2)$ intersections. We denote by $\hat{\theta} = \left\{\boldsymbol{\theta}_i^u, \boldsymbol{\theta}_i^d\right\}_{i=1}^k$ the set of all curves.

We then compute the arrangement of pseudolines $A(\hat{\theta})$ as follows. The bounding box of $A(\hat{\theta})$ defined by $\theta = -\frac{1}{2}\pi$, $\theta = \frac{1}{2}\pi$ and two values of α, one is smaller than the smallest α value of all the intersections, and the second is larger than the largest α value of all the intersections. All the curves $\hat{\theta}$ that intersect the bounding box form an arrangement of pseudolines (we assume that not all the switch events occur simultaneously — this can be detected in $O(k^2)$ time). We then compute the pseudoline arrangement $A(\hat{\theta})$, which takes $O(k^2)$ time (follows from Theorem 3.3).

Table 3.1 lists an algorithm to compute the uncertainty envelope of an LPGUM line. We examine the values of α from the smallest value before the first event to the largest value after the last event. As α changes, the point zonotope $l_\alpha(q)$ slides along the line, tracing out the line's envelope (Fig. 2.1(b)). The sweep stops at intersection points. At each stop, we find the relevant switch events based on the pseudolines' arrangement structure. The algorithm iterates over all the events, tracing out the upper and lower segment chain.

To find an initial value for α (Table 3.1, line 2), we compute all flip events and add them to the event queue in $O(k \log k)$ time. We set α to be the smallest value. To find the first switch event in the pseudoline arrangement, we traverse all the lines, and for each line, we find the value of α for which the first intersection with the current line occurs. Then, we check for twist events for this value of α, add them to the event queue and set α to the smallest value of these events. Finding this initial value takes $O(k \log k)$ time since there are at most k flip events. Finding the first switch event in the pseudolines' arrangement takes $O(k)$ time since there are at most k twist events.

We handle the events as described in Section 3.2.1. We find the relevant twist and switch events during the line sweep (Table 3.1, lines 3b and 3c). For the switch events, after each flip or relevant twist or switch event, we examine the lines of the cone diagram that define the current supporting vertex, or the vertices of the current supporting segment — no more than four vertices are defined by six lines of the cone diagram. For each line in the cone diagram, we locate the corresponding line in the pseudoline arrangement and find the first intersection for a value of α larger than the value of α in the previous event. We also test for relevant twist events of the supporting vertex or of the vertices of the current supporting segment and retrieve the next flip event from the event queue. We handle the event with the smallest value of α. When the event is not a flip event, we insert the flip event back to the queue (Table 3.1, line 3d). The algorithm terminates when the event queue is empty and there are no more relevant switch or twist events. The outputs are the upper and lower line envelope segment chains.

Theorem 3.4. *The uncertainty envelope of an LPGUM line $l(q)$, defined over a parametric uncertainty model $(q, \bar{q}, \Delta)$ of k parameters, can be computed in $O(k^2)$ time and space.*

Proof. The algorithm correctness follows directly from Theorem 3.3 and Lemma 3.5. The $O(k^2)$ time and space complexity is determined by the pseudoline arrangement computation. Computing the initial value for α and inserting all flip events in the event queue

(Table 3.1, line 2) require $O(k \log k)$ time. Computing the next relevant switch and twist events (Table 3.1, lines 3b, 3c) requires constant time using the pseudoline arrangement structure. Handling all relevant twist events, relevant switch events and flip events (Table 3.1, line 3e) requires $O(k)$ time, as there are $O(k)$ such events and each is handled in constant time. Note that each switch event requires updating the two cones on the cone diagram in constant time.   □

3.3   LPGUM Three-Point Circle

We now describe an efficient algorithm for computing the envelope of an LPGUM three-point circle in $O(k^2)$ time. First, we describe an algorithm to detect if a three-point circle spans the entire plane. Next, we describe the properties of the outer envelope of an independent LPGUM three-point circle. Finally, we describe an algorithm to compute the LPGUM three-point circle envelope.

3.3.1   LPGUM three-point circle spanning the plane

We describe next two methods for detecting if a three-point circle union CU_{uvw} spans the entire plane — one for the independent case and one for the dependent case.

Independent case: Consider first the zonotopes of two disjoint LPGUM points $u(q)$ and $v(q)$. Then, when point $w(q)$ is above or below (left or right) all four tangent lines, due to the zonotopes' convexity, no three point instances can lie on a line, so CU_{uvw} does not cover the entire plane. The inner and outer tangents' computation and the testing of whether point $w(q)$ is above or below the four tangent lines require $O(k)$ time each.

Dependent case: Three LPGUM points $u(q) = \overline{u} + qA_u$, $v(q) = \overline{v} + qA_v$, $w(q) = \overline{w} + qA_w$ where $A_u = (d_{ux}, d_{uy})$, $A_v = (d_{vx}, d_{vy})$, $A_w = (d_{wx}, d_{wy})$ are collinear when $\exists \alpha, \beta \in \mathbb{R}$ and $\exists q_a \in \Delta$ so that $\alpha x + \beta y = 1$:

$$\begin{cases} \alpha d_{ux}(q_a) + \beta d_{uy}(q_a) = 1 \\ \alpha d_{vx}(q_a) + \beta d_{vy}(q_a) = 1 \\ \alpha d_{wx}(q_a) + \beta d_{wy}(q_a) = 1 \end{cases}$$

and

$$\begin{cases} \alpha(\bar{d}_{ux} + q_a(A_u)_{*,x}) + \beta(\bar{d}_{uy} + q_a(A_u)_{*,y}) = 1 \\ \alpha(\bar{d}_{vx} + q_a(A_v)_{*,x}) + \beta(\bar{d}_{vy} + q_a(A_v)_{*,y}) = 1 \\ \alpha(\bar{d}_{wx} + q_a(A_w)_{*,x}) + \beta(\bar{d}_{wy} + q_a(A_w)_{*,y}) = 1 \end{cases}$$

The solution of this linear problem with quadratic constraints with unknown α, β and q_a equations determines if the points are collinear. It can be solved by quadratic programming.

We present next a more efficient geometric solution with time complexity of $O(k^2)$. First, we describe how to determine the direction of two disjoint LPGUM points and then we describe how to determine the orientation of three disjoint LPGUM points.

Let $u(q)$ and $v(q)$ be two points and let $\vec{r}(q) = u(q) - v(q)$ be the uncertain direction vector from $v(q)$ to $u(q)$, i.e., $\vec{r}(q) = \vec{r} + qA_r$, where $\vec{r} = \bar{u} - \bar{v}$ and $A_r = A_u - A_v$ represent all possible vectors from $v(q)$ to $u(q)$. A **direction flip** between $u(q)$ and $v(q)$ occurs iff there exist $q_a, q_b \in \Delta$ such that

$$\langle \vec{r}(q_a), \vec{r}(q_b) \rangle < 0$$

If one of the vectors is the nominal direction from $v(q)$ to $u(q)$, i.e., $\vec{r} = \bar{u} - \bar{v}$, we say that there is a direction flip with respect to the nominal direction or a nominal direction flip (Fig. 3.6). An instance of $\vec{r}(q)$ that is flipped with respect to $\vec{r}$ is identified by finding q_c such that $\langle \vec{r}(q_c), \vec{r} \rangle < 0$. To compute q_c, we solve

$$q_c = \arg\max_{q \in \Delta} \langle \vec{r}(q), -\vec{r} \rangle < 0$$

in $O(k)$ time by computing $a_j = \langle (A_r)_{j,*}, \vec{r} \rangle$ for every column of A_r. If $a_j \leq 0$, set the j parameter of q_c to q_j^+, else set it to q_j^-.

To solve the general direction flip query, we compute the uncertainty envelope of $\vec{r}(q)$ by treating $\vec{r}(q)$ as an LPGUM point. Let l be a line tangent to $Z(\vec{r}(q))$ going through the origin. If the line perpendicular to l going through the origin intersects $Z(\vec{r}(q))$, then there is a direction flip. Note that if a straight line intersects a convex polygon, there are vertices of the polygon on both sides of the line. Let $\vec{r}(q_d)$ be an instance that has its endpoint on l. A representative instance of a vector that is flipped with respect to $\vec{r}(q_d)$ is computed by inspecting all the vertices of the zonotope. If the origin is in the

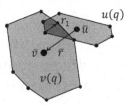

Fig. 3.6.   Direction of two uncertain points $u(q)$ and $v(q)$ with nominal locations $\bar{u}$ and $\bar{v}$, and nominal direction $\bar{r}$, and point uncertainty zones (gray). Direction vector r_1 shows a direction flip with respect to $\bar{r}$.

interior of the zonotope, there is a direction flip with respect to all vectors.

Theorem 3.5. *Let $u(q)$ and $v(q)$ be two points, and let $\vec{r}(q) = u(q) - v(q)$ be the uncertain direction vector from $v(q)$ to $u(q)$. There is a direction flip with respect to any direction iff the origin lies in $Z(\vec{r}(q))$.*

Proof.   When the origin is in the interior of the uncertainty envelope, then for every instance $\vec{r}(q_a)$ there is an instance $\vec{r}(q_b)$ such that $\vec{r}(q_a) = -a\vec{r}(q_b)$ for some $a \in \mathbb{R}$. Thus, there is a direction flip for every instance of $\vec{r}(q)$.

We prove the opposite direction by contradiction. Assume by contradiction that there is a direction flip with respect to any direction, but the origin does not lie in the interior of the envelope. Let l_1 and l_2 be two lines tangent to the envelope of $\vec{r}(q)$ and going through the origin, and let $l_1^{\perp}$ and $l_2^{\perp}$ be the lines perpendicular to l_1 and l_2, respectively, going through the origin (Fig. 3.7). Since the origin is not in the interior of the zonotope, there exists an instance $\vec{r}(q_a)$ of $\vec{r}(q)$ that lies in the cone defined by $l_1^{\perp}$ and $l_2^{\perp}$. The line perpendicular to $\vec{r}(q_a)$ going through the origin lies in the double wedge defined by l_1 and l_2 and thus will not intersect the zonotope. This implies that there is no instance of $\vec{r}(q)$ that is flipped with respect to $\vec{r}(q_a)$.   □

Theorem 3.6. *Let $u(q)$ and $v(q)$ be two points such that the origin does not lie in the interior of the uncertainty envelope of $\vec{r}(q) = u(q) - v(q)$. Let l_1 and l_2 be two distinct lines tangent to $\vec{r}(q)$ going*

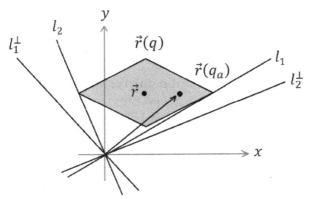

Fig. 3.7. Example of a point instance that has no flipped counterpart. The lines l_1 and l_2 are two lines tangent to the envelope of $\vec{r}(q)$ that go through the origin. Lines $l_1^{\perp}$ and $l_2^{\perp}$ are lines perpendicular to l_1 and l_2, respectively, that go through the origin. The vector $\vec{r}(q_a)$ is an example of an instance of $\vec{r}(q)$ that has no other instance flipped with respect to it.

through the origin and let $\vec{r}(q_a)$ and $\vec{r}(q_b)$ be two instances that lie on l_1 and l_2, respectively. There is a general direction flip iff $\langle \vec{r}(q_a), \vec{r}(q_b) \rangle < 0$.

Proof. If $\langle \vec{r}(q_a), \vec{r}(q_b) \rangle < 0$, then there is by definition a direction flip.

Conversely, if there is a direction flip, there exist two instances $\vec{r}(q_c)$ and $\vec{r}(q_d)$ such that $\langle \vec{r}(q_c), \vec{r}(q_d) \rangle < 0$. By construction, $\vec{r}(q_c)$ and $\vec{r}(q_d)$ are in the cone defined by $\vec{r}(q_a)$ and $\vec{r}(q_b)$ and thus also $\langle \vec{r}(q_a), \vec{r}(q_b) \rangle < 0$. $\qquad\square$

By Theorems 3.5 and 3.6, to answer a general flip query, we must first test if the origin lies in the interior of the envelope of $\vec{r}(q)$. If it does not, we find two instances $\vec{r}(q_a)$ and $\vec{r}(q_b)$ such that the lines along them are distinct and are both tangent to the envelope. If $\langle \vec{r}(q_a), \vec{r}(q_b) \rangle < 0$, there is a direction flip, otherwise there is not.

Computing the envelope of $\vec{r}(q)$ takes $O(k \log k)$ time. Testing if the origin lies in it takes $O(\log k)$ time, and computing $\vec{r}(q_a)$ and $\vec{r}(q_b)$ takes $O(k)$ time.

Theorem 3.7. *Let* $u(q), v(q)$ *and* $w(q)$ *be three points. An orientation flip among* $u(q), v(q)$ *and* $w(q)$ *can be detected in* $O(k^2)$ *time.*

Proof.   First, we compute $\vec{r}(q) = u(q) - v(q)$ and $\vec{s}(q) = w(q) - v(q)$. There is an orientation flip among the points $u(q), v(q)$ and $w(q)$ iff there is an orientation flip among $\vec{r}(q), \vec{s}(q)$ and the origin while treating $\vec{r}(q), \vec{s}(q)$ as points.

Next, $\vec{r}(q)$ and $\vec{s}(q)$ can be interpreted as endpoints of an uncertain line segment. The uncertainty envelope of an uncertain line/segment is computed in $O(k^2)$ time. For every point in the proper interior of an uncertain line, there exists at least one pair of lines such that the point is to the left of one and to the right of the other. Thus, if the origin is in the proper interior of the uncertain line connecting $\vec{r}(q)$ and $\vec{s}(q)$, there is an orientation flip among the points. If a point lies outside the uncertainty zone of an uncertain line, then it is to one side of all the instances of the line. Hence, if the origin lies outside the line connecting $\vec{r}(q)$ and $\vec{s}(q)$, there is no orientation flip.

Determining if a point is in the interior of an uncertain line takes $O(\log k)$ time. Therefore, the time necessary to determine if there is an orientation flip is $O(k^2)$.   □

3.3.2   The outer envelope of an independent LPGUM three-point circle

We describe next the properties of the outer envelope of an independent LPGUM three-point circle. Figure 3.8 shows two examples of LPGUM circle instances defined by three LPGUM points and their relation to the LPGUM point uncertainty zones.

Theorem 3.8. *The outer envelope of an independent LPGUM three-point circle $c_{uvw}(q)$ consists of three arc segments corresponding to three instances of the parameter vector $q_a, q_b, q_c \in \Delta$: outer_arc $(c_{uvw}(q_b))$, outer_arc$(c_{uvw}(q_c))$, outer_arc$(c_{uvw}(q_d))$ (Section 2.5).*

Proof.   Follows from Lemmas 3.6–3.9.   □

Lemma 3.6. *None of the circle instances*

$$c_{uvw}(q_a) = circle(u(q_a), v(q_a), w(q_a))$$

such that outer_arc$(c_{uvw}(q_a)) \in \partial CU_{uvw}$ *intersect the zonotopes* $U = \langle p_{u1}, p_{u2}, \ldots, p_{uK} \rangle$, $V = \langle p_{v1}, p_{v2}, \ldots, p_{vK} \rangle$ *and* $W = \langle p_{w1}, p_{w2}, \ldots, p_{wK} \rangle$.

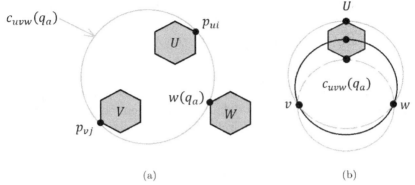

(a)　　　　　　　　　　　(b)

Fig. 3.8. Illustration of three-point circle instances defined by three LPGUM points: (a) a circle instance $c_{uvw}(q_a)$ defined by point instances p_{ui}, p_{vj} and $w(q_a)$; zonotopes U, V are inside $c_{uvw}(q_a)$ and zonotope W is outside $c_{uvw}(q_a)$; (b) a circle instance $c_{uvw}(q_a)$ that intersects zonotope U. Circle $c_{uvw}(q_a)$ is defined by an LPGUM point $u(q)$ and two exact points v, w. In gray are circle instances such that $c_{uvw}(q_a)$ is inside their envelope (gray continuous line).

Proof. Assume by contradiction that the circle instance

$$c_{uvw}(q_a) = \text{outer\_arc}(c_{uvw}(q_a)) \in \partial CU_{uvw}$$

intersects zonotope U. Then, there exist two circle instances such that $c_{uvw}(q_a)$ is inside their envelope. Figure 3.8 illustrates this situation. Therefore,

$$\text{outer\_arc}(c_{uvw}(q_a)) \notin \partial CU_{uvw}$$

Consequently, the three points $u(q_a), v(q_a), w(q_a)$ that define circle instance $c_{uvw}(q_a)$ such that $\text{outer\_arc}(c_{uvw}(q_a)) \in \partial CU_{uvw}$ are tangent to the zonotopes at a vertex or are on an edge: $u(q_a) \in \partial Z(u(q)), v(q_a) \in \partial Z(v(q)), w(q_a) \in \partial Z(w(q))$. □

Lemma 3.7. *A zonotope $U = \langle p_{u1}, p_{u2}, \ldots, p_{uK} \rangle$ is inside circle instance $c_{uvw}(q_a)$ iff every vertex that defined it, $\forall p_{ui} \in U$, is inside $c_{uvw}(q_a)$. The proof is straightforward.*

Lemma 3.8. *When a zonotope $U = \langle p_{u1}, p_{u2}, \ldots, p_{uK} \rangle$ is inside a circle instance $c_{uvw}(q_a)$ such that U is tangent to $c_{uvw}(q_a)$ at point $u(q_a)$, then $u(q_a)$ is a vertex of zonotope U.*

Proof.   By contradiction, assume that U is inside $c_{uvw}(q_a)$ such that U is tangent to $c_{uvw}(q_a)$ at point $u(q_a) \in \partial Z(u(q))$, but $u(q_a) \notin U$. Then, $u(q_a)$ is on an edge e_{uij} of zonotope U that is tangent to $c_{uvw}(q_a)$.

The endpoints of edge e_{uij} are vertices $p_{ui}, p_{uj} \in U$, $j = (i+1)_{mod\,K}$. Zonotope U is inside $c_{uvw}(q_a)$, so points p_{ui}, p_{uj} are inside $c_{uvw}(q_a)$. However, by definition, a tangent to a circle has only one common point with the circle. This is a contradiction.   □

Lemma 3.9. *Each circle instance* $c_{uvw}(q_a) = \mathrm{outer\_arc}(c_{uvw}(q_a)) \in \partial CU_{uvw}$ *contains two zonotopes* $U = \langle p_{u1}, p_{u2}, \ldots, p_{uK} \rangle$ *and* $V = \langle p_{v1}, p_{v2}, \ldots, p_{vK} \rangle$.

Proof.   By Lemma 3.6, every circle instance $c_{uvw}(q_a)$, s.t. $\mathrm{outer\_arc}(c_{uvw}(q_a)) \in \partial CU_{uvw}$, is tangent to zonotopes U, V, W. This yields four cases (Figs. 3.9 and 3.10):

Case 1: Zonotopes U, V, W are outside the circle $c_{uvw}(q_a)$.

Case 2: Zonotopes U, V, W are inside the circle $c_{uvw}(q_a)$.

Case 3: Zonotope U is inside the circle $c_{uvw}(q_a)$ and zonotopes V, W are outside the circle $c_{uvw}(q_a)$.

Case 4: Zonotopes U, V are inside the circle $c_{uvw}(q_a)$ and zonotope W is outside the circle $c_{uvw}(q_a)$.

For Cases 1–3 (Fig. 3.9(a)–(c)), by convexity and Thales's theorem, there exist circle instances such that $c_{uvw}(q_a)$ is inside

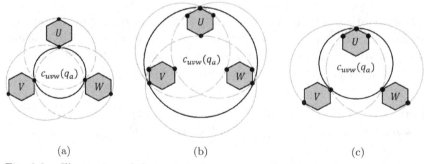

(a)   (b)   (c)

Fig. 3.9.   Illustration of Cases 1–3. In gray are circle instances such that circle instance $c_{uvw}(q_a)$ is inside their envelope (gray continuous line); (a) Case 1: zonotopes U, V, W are outside $c_{uvw}(q_a)$; (b) Case 2: zonotopes U, V, W are inside $c_{uvw}(q_a)$; (c) Case 3: zonotope U are inside $c_{uvw}(q_a)$.

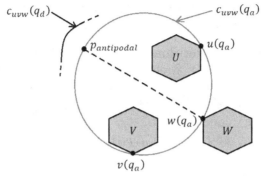

Fig. 3.10.   Case 4: Illustration of a circle instance $c_{uvw}(q_a)$ (gray circle) defined by point instances $u(q_a), v(q_a), w(q_a)$. Zonotopes U, V are inside $c_{uvw}(q_a)$ and W is outside $c_{uvw}(q_a)$. In black are point $p_{\text{antipodal}}$ and part of a circle instance $c_{uvw}(q_d)$. The black dotted line is the diameter of $c_{uvw}(q_a)$. Circle $c_{uvw}(q_d)$ cannot be placed to the right of point $p_{\text{antipodal}}$ in counterclockwise order.

their envelope. For Case 4 (Fig. 3.10), assume by contradiction that outer_arc($c_{uvw}(q_a)$) $\notin \partial CU_{uvw}$. Then, the outer envelope $\partial(\text{outer\_arc}(c_{uvw}(q_b)) \cup \text{outer\_arc}(c_{uvw}(q_c)) \cup \text{outer\_arc}(c_{uvw}(q_d)))$ is such that $c_{uvw}(q_a)$ is placed inside:

$$\partial(\text{outer\_arc}(c_{uvw}(q_b)) \cup \text{outer\_arc}(c_{uvw}(q_c)) \cup \text{outer\_arc}(c_{uvw}(q_d)))$$

Let $p_{\text{antipodal}}$ be the antipodal point of $w(q_a)$ on $c_{uvw}(q_a)$ (Fig. 3.10). Since outer_arc($c_{uvw}(q_a)$) $\notin \partial CU_{uvw}$, there is an arc segment to the right of $p_{\text{antipodal}}$ in counterclockwise order. Let $c_{uvw}(q_d)$ be the circle to which the arc belongs. Let $c_{uvw}(q_d)$ be defined by points $u(q_d), v(q_d), w(q_d)$. Then, at least one of the following three statements holds:

1. Point $u(q_d)$ is outside the circle $c_{uvw}(q_a)$.
2. Point $v(q_d)$ is outside the circle $c_{uvw}(q_a)$.
3. Point $w(q_d)$ is inside the circle $c_{uvw}(q_a)$.

Circle $c_{uvw}(q_a)$ is tangent to U, V, W and W is outside $c_{uvw}(q_a)$, so point $w(q_d)$ is outside $c_{uvw}(q_a)$. Zonotopes U, V are inside $c_{uvw}(q_a)$, so points $u(q_d), v(q_d)$ are inside circle instance $c_{uvw}(q_a)$. This is a contradiction.   □

3.3.3 Algorithm to compute the outer envelope of an independent LPGUM three-point circle

We describe next an algorithm for computing the outer envelope of an independent LPGUM three-point circle. Following Theorem 3.8 and Lemmas 3.6–3.9, we formulate the geometric problem of finding the outer envelope of an LPGUM circle $c_{uvw}(q)$ as follows.

Given three zonotopes $U = \langle p_{u1}, p_{u2}, \ldots, p_{uK} \rangle$, $V = \langle p_{v1}, p_{v2}, \ldots, p_{vK} \rangle$ and $W = \langle p_{w1}, p_{w2}, \ldots, p_{wK} \rangle$, compute the three tangent circle instances such that

1. $c_{uvw}(q_a) = circle(p_{ui}, p_{vj}, w(q_a)), p_{ui} \in U, p_{vj} \in V, w(q_a) \in \partial Z(w(q))$ where U and V are inside $c_{uvw}(q_a)$ and W is outside of it.
2. $c_{uvw}(q_b) = circle(p_{ui}, v(q_b), p_{wl}), p_{ui} \in U, v(q_b) \in \partial Z(v(q)), p_{wl} \in W$ where U and W are inside $c_{uvw}(q_b)$ and V is outside of it.
3. $c_{uvw}(q_c) = circle(u(q_c), p_{vj}, p_{wl}), u(q_c) \in \partial Z(u(q)), p_{vj} \in V, p_{wl} \in W$ where V and W are inside $c_{uvw}(q_c)$ and U is outside of it.

We describe next an algorithm for computing one of these circles, $c_{uvw}(q_a)$ — the other two cases are similar. First, we define the smallest three-point enclosing circle problem as the smallest circle enclosing the three zonotopes such that it is tangent to each zonotope. Next, we describe an algorithm to test if a circle is tangent to an edge or to one of its vertices. Finally, we describe an algorithm for computing the outer envelope of the uncertainty zone.

3.3.3.1 *Smallest three-point enclosing circle*

Assume first that point $w(q_a)$ is given. The goal is to find vertices p_{ui}, p_{vj}. By Lemma 3.7, we know that if $\forall p_{ui} \in U, \forall p_{vj} \in V$ are inside $c_{uvw}(q_a)$, then U and V are also inside $c_{uvw}(q_a)$. Therefore, $c_{uvw}(q_a)$ is the smallest three-point enclosing circle with points $p_{ui} \in U, p_{vj} \in V, w(q_a)$ on its envelope.

The algorithm for computing the smallest three-point enclosing circle is based on the algorithm for finding the smallest enclosing disk described in Ref. [62]. It consists of three cases:

Case 1: point $w(q_a)$ is given. The goal is to find points $p_{ui} \in U, p_{vj} \in V$ such that the circle defined by the three points is the smallest three-point enclosing circle.

Case 2: two points $w(q_a)$ and $p_{ui} \in U$ on the smallest three-point enclosing circle are given. The goal is to find the third point $p_{vj} \in V$.

Case 3: two points $w(q_a)$ and $p_{vj} \in V$ on the smallest three-point enclosing circle are given. The goal is to find the third point $p_{ui} \in U$.

Let $P = \{p_1, \ldots, p_n\}$ be a permutation of all vertices of zonotopes U, V. The algorithm sequentially adds the points while maintaining the smallest three-point enclosing circle C_i of the i points.

The algorithm **Min-Circle-1-Point**(P, w) listed in Table 3.2 handles Case 1 for $w = w(q_a)$. The algorithm **Min-Circle-2-Points**(P, v, w) listed in Table 3.3 handles Case 2 where P includes the $l - 1$ added points, $v = p_l$ and $w = w(q_a)$. It also handles Case 3 with u replacing v, Min-Circle-2-Points(P, u, w).

The correctness of the algorithms directly follows the following Lemma.

Lemma 3.10. *Let P be a set of points in the plane, let R be a disjoint, possibly empty set of points $P \cap R = \emptyset$, and let $p \in P$. Denote by $mc(P, R)$ the smallest three-point enclosing circle that encloses P and has all points of R on its boundary. Then the following holds:*

1. *If $p \in mc(P - \{p\}, R)$, then $mc(P, R) = mc(P - \{p\}, R)$.*
2. *If $p \notin mc(P - \{p\}, R)$, then $mc(P, R) = mc(P, R \cup \{p\})$.*

Proof.

1. When $p \in mc(P - \{p\}, R)$, then $mc(P - \{p\}, R)$ contains P and has R on its boundary. There cannot be any smaller circle containing P with R on its boundary because such a circle would also be a containing circle for $P - \{p\}$ with R on its boundary, contradicting the definition of $mc(P - \{p\}, R)$. Consequently, $mc(P, R) = mc(P - \{p\}, R)$.
2. Let $D(0) = mc(P - \{p\}, R)$ and $D(1) = mc(P, R \cup \{p\})$ with centers $x(0)$ and $x(1)$, respectively. We define a continuous family $\{D(\lambda) | 0 \leq \lambda \leq 1\}$ of circles as follows (Fig. 3.11). Let z be an intersection point of $\partial D(0)$ and $\partial D(1)$, the envelopes of $D(0)$ and $D(1)$. The center of $D(\lambda)$ is the point $x(\lambda) = (1 - \lambda)x(0) + \lambda x(1)$ and the radius of $D(\lambda)$ is $d(x(\lambda), z)$, so the family defines a continuous deformation of $D(0)$ to $D(1)$. By the assumption, $p \notin D(0)$ and $p \in D(1)$, so by continuity there must exist a $0 < \lambda^* \leq 1$ such that p lies on the boundary of $D(\lambda^*)$. Thus,

Table 3.2.   Algorithm for computing the smallest three-point circle with point w on its envelope.

Min-Circle-1-Point(P, w)

Input: A set P of n points in the plane and a point w such that there exists a three-point enclosing circle for P with $p_{ui} \in U, p_{vj} \in V$ and w on its envelope.

1. Compute a random permutation $\{p_1, \ldots, p_n\}$ of P.
2. Save pointers to the first $p_i \in U$ and $p_j \in V$ in the above permutation.
3. Replace them with points p_1 and p_2.
4. Let C_1 be a three-point circle defined by p_1, p_2 and w.
5. for $l \leftarrow 3$ to n

    a. **do if** $p_l \in C_{l-1}$
          then $C_l \leftarrow C_{l-1}$
    b. **else if** $p_l \in V$ **then** $C_l \leftarrow$ **Min-Circle-2-Points**($\{p_1, \ldots, p_{l-1}\}, p_l, w$)
    c. **else if** $p_l \in U$ **then** $C_l \leftarrow$ **Min-Circle-2-Points**($\{p_1, \ldots, p_{l-1}\}, p_l, w$)

6. **return** C_n

Output: The smallest three-point enclosing circle of P defined by $p_{ui} \in U, p_{vj} \in V$ and w.

Table 3.3.   Algorithm for computing the smallest three-point circle, with w and u on its envelope.

Min-Circle-2-Points(P, u, w)

Input: A set P of n points in the plane and two points u, w such that there exists a three-point enclosing circle for P defined by u, w and $p_j \in V$.

1. Initialization: $p_1 \leftarrow$ first $p_j \in V$ in P and $C_1 \leftarrow$ three-point circle defined by u, w, p_1.
2. **for** $i \leftarrow 2$ to n
3. **do if** $p_i \in V$

    a. **do if** $p_i \in C_{i-1}$
          then $C_i \leftarrow C_{i-1}$
    b. **else** $C_j \leftarrow$ three-point circle defined by u, w, p_j.

4. **return** C_n

Output: The smallest three-point enclosing circle for P defined by w, u and $p_j \in V$.

$P \subset D(\lambda^*)$ and $R \subset \partial D(\lambda^*)$. Since the radius of any $D(\lambda^*)$ with $0 < \lambda < 1$ is strictly smaller than the radius of $D(1)$, and $D(1)$ is by definition the smallest enclosing circle for P, we must have $\lambda^* = 1$. In other words, $D(1)$ has p on its boundary. $\qquad \square$

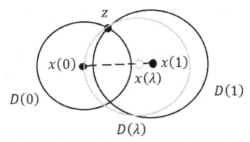

Fig. 3.11. Illustration of the continuous deformation of disk $D(0)$ into circles $D(1)$; points $x(0)$ and $x(1)$ are the centers of $D(0)$ and $D(1)$, z is an intersection point of the envelopes of the disks $\partial D(0)$ and $\partial D(1)$. $D(\lambda)$ is a disk defined by the radius $x(\lambda)$ and point z on its envelope.

Theorem 3.9. *The smallest three-point enclosing circle for a set of n points in the plane can be computed in $O(n)$ expected time using worst-case linear storage.*

Proof. **Min-Circle-2-Points**(P,v,w) and **Min-Circle-2-Points** (P,u,w) run in $O(n)$ time because every iteration of the loop takes constant time with $O(n)$ storage.

Min-Circle-1-Point(P, w) also requires $O(n)$ space and its expected running time is $O(n)$ excluding the time for calls to **Min-Circle-2-Points**(P,v,w) and **Min-Circle-2-Points**(P,u,w). To show this, we use backward analysis to bound this probability: fix a subset $\{p_1, \ldots, p_l\}$, and let C_i be the smallest three-point circle enclosing $\{p_1, \ldots, p_i\}$ with w on its boundary. The smallest enclosing circle changes only when one of the three points is removed from the boundary. One of the points on the boundary is w, so there are at most two points that cause the smallest enclosing circle to shrink. The probability that p_i is one of those points is $2/i$. So, the total expected running time of **Min-Circle-1-Point**(P, w) is

$$O(n) + \sum_{i=2}^{n} O(i)\frac{2}{i} = O(n)$$

thus, the expected running time is $O(n)$. □

Theorem 3.10. *The smallest three-point enclosing circle for a set of n points in the plane can be computed in $O(n)$ expected time and space.*

3.3.3.2   *Circle tangent to an edge or to one of its vertices test*

We describe next the procedure for testing if a given vertex $p_{wl} \in W$ or its neighboring edges $e_{(l-1 \bmod K)l}, e_{l(l+1 \bmod K)}$ defined by neighboring vertices $p_{w(l-1 \bmod K)}, p_{w(l+1 \bmod K)}$ are tangent to circle $c_{uvw}(q_a)$ where $K \le 2k - 1$ is the number of segments in the edge envelope.

Lemma 3.11. *Let $c_{uvw}(q_a) = \mathrm{circle}(u(q_a), v(q_a), w(q_a))$ be a circle that intersects zonotope U. Then, the point $u(q_b)$ that defines the circle tangent to U, so that U is outside $c_{uvw}(q_b)$, is inside $c_{uvw}(q_a)$.*

Figure 3.8(b) illustrates this situation. The proof relies on convexity and is straightforward.

First, note that the zonotope that is outside and tangent to a circle has only one common point with the circle. Thus, if one of its neighbor vertices $p_{w(l-1 \bmod K)}, p_{w(l+1 \bmod K)}$ is inside the circle, then vertex p_{wl} is not tangent to the circle. When both neighbors $p_{w(l-1 \bmod K)}, p_{w(l+1 \bmod K)}$ are outside $c_{uvw}(q_a)$ and one of the edges $e_{(l-1 \bmod K)l}, e_{l(l+1 \bmod K)}$ intersects it, then by Lemma 3.11, the tangent point lies on this edge. When both neighbors $p_{w(l-1 \bmod K)}, p_{w(l+1 \bmod K)}$ are outside $c_{uvw}(q_a)$ and both edges $e_{(l-1 \bmod K)l}, e_{l(l+1 \bmod K)}$ do not intersect $c_{uvw}(q_a)$, then vertex p_{wl} is tangent to $c_{uvw}(q_a)$. Since the number of steps is constant, the time complexity of the procedure is $O(1)$. The correctness of this procedure follows directly from Lemma 3.11.

3.3.3.3   *Outer envelope of an LPGUM three-point circle*

We now complete the algorithm for finding the outer envelope of an LPGUM three-point circle. We first prove Lemma 3.12 and then describe a procedure for finding a tangent point $w(q_a) \in \partial Z(w(q))$.

Lemma 3.12. *A zonotope W has a single vertex tangent to circle $c_{uvw}(q_a)$ such that U, V, W are inside $c_{uvw}(q_a)$.*

Proof.   Assume by contradiction that there are two such vertices, p_{ui} and p_{uj}. Let $c_{uvw}(q_a) = \mathrm{circle}(p_{ui}, p_{vm}, p_{wn})$ and $c_{uvw}(q_b) = \mathrm{circle}(p_{uj}, p_{ve}, p_{wf})$ be their corresponding circles (Fig. 3.12).

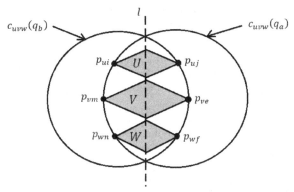

Fig. 3.12. Illustration of two circle instances $c_{uvw}(q_a) = \text{circle}(p_{ui}, p_{vm}, p_{wn})$ and $c_{uvw}(q_b) = \text{circle}(p_{uj}, p_{ve}, p_{wf})$ tangent to zonotopes U, V, W (gray parallelograms) inside $c_{uvw}(q_a), c_{uvw}(q_b)$. Line l passes through the two intersection points of the circles (black dotted line).

Circles $c_{uvw}(q_a)$ and $c_{uvw}(q_b)$ contain U, V, W so $U, V, W \subseteq c_{uvw}(q_a) \bigcap c_{uvw}(q_b)$, and $c_{uvw}(q_a)$ and $c_{uvw}(q_b)$ intersect. Let l be the line that passes through the two intersection points of $c_{uvw}(q_a)$ and $c_{uvw}(q_b)$. By definition, vertices p_{ui}, p_{vm}, p_{wn} are on $c_{uvw}(q_a)$ and vertices p_{uj}, p_{ve}, p_{wf} are on $c_{uvw}(q_b)$. Since U, V, W are zonotopes and $p_{ui}, p_{uj} \in U, p_{vm}, p_{ve} \in V, p_{wn}, p_{wf} \in W$, line l intersects zonotopes U, V, W. This is a contradiction to the assumption that no three points are collinear in all point set instances. □

Lemma 3.12 also holds for the case when U, V are inside $c_{uvw}(q_a)$ and W is outside of it (the proof is similar). Note that point $w(q_a)$ can be a vertex in W or can lie on one of its edges.

We find the point $w(q_a)$ by a binary search as follows. Let l denote the line that passes through the vertices $p_{w1}, p_{w(\frac{K}{2})}$ of W. First, we divide W into two parts, one to the left of line l and the other to the right of it. To determine in which of the two parts tangent point $w(q_a)$ is present, we compute the two smallest enclosing three-point circles that contain all the vertices of zonotopes U, V where p_{w1} defines the boundary of the first circle $c_{uvw}(q_a) = \text{circle}(p_{ui}, p_{vm}, p_{w1})$, and $p_{w(\frac{K}{2})}$ defines the boundary of the second circle $c_{uvw}(q_b) = circle(p_{uj}, p_{ve}, p_{w(\frac{K}{2})})$.

Table 3.4.   Summary of the results for elementary LPGUM geometric entities.

Entity	Uncertain envelope	Complexity	
		Time	Space
Coordinate	Interval	$\theta(k)$	$O(1)$
Point	Zonotope	$\theta(k \log k)$	$O(k)$
Line	Chain of line and parabola segments	$O(k^2)$	$O(k)$
Independent three-point circle	Three arc segments	Expected $O(k \log k)$	$O(1)$

When vertex p_{w1} or one of its neighbor edges is tangent to $c_{uvw}(q_a)$, or when vertex $p_{w(\frac{K}{2})}$ or one of his neighbor edges is tangent to circle $c_{uvw}(q_b)$, then we have found the tangent. Otherwise, by Lemma 3.7, at least one of the neighbor vertices of p_{w1} is inside $c_{uvw}(q_a)$ or one of the neighbor vertices of $p_{w(\frac{K}{2})}$ is inside $c_{uvw}(q_b)$.

Consequently, by Lemma 3.11, the tangent point lies on the side of the vertex that is inside the corresponding circle. This determines the part of W that is tangent to $w(q_a)$. Similarly, we divide the part in which $w(q_a)$ is into two parts and test in which of them $w(q_a)$ lies. This is repeated until we find $w(q_a)$.

Note that the point $w(q_a)$ can be a vertex in W or can be on one of its edges. In this case, the procedure that finds the smallest three-point enclosing circle can be modified as follows. Instead of computing the circle with three points, we compute it with two points and a line tangent to the circle. The correctness of this procedure follows from Lemmas 3.11 and 3.12.

Theorem 3.11. *Computing the three circles that form the outer envelope of an LPGUM three-point circle, i.e., the circle instances $c_{uvw}(q_a), c_{uvw}(q_b), c_{uvw}(q_c)$ for $q_a, q_b, q_c \in \Delta$, requires $O(k \log k)$ expected time.*

Proof.   Since there are $O(k)$ vertices in zonotope W, a binary search requires $O(\log k)$ iterations, each of which calls the smallest three-point enclosing circle procedure once, which takes $O(k)$

expected time (Theorem 3.9). Since the other steps require constant time, the total expected running time is $O(k \log k)$. $\square$

3.4   Summary

In this chapter, we described algorithms to compute the uncertainty envelope of points, lines and circles. We have also presented proofs for the complexity of their envelopes and for the time needed to compute them. In all cases, the additional cost for computing using LPGUM in both time and space is a low polynomial (Table 3.4).

Chapter 4

Half-Plane Point Retrieval Queries

This chapter addresses a family of geometric half-plane retrieval queries of points in the plane in the presence of geometric uncertainty. The problems include exact and uncertain point sets and half-plane queries defined by an exact or uncertain line. Section 4.1 introduces the problem. Section 4.2 defines the half-plane retrieval queries and presents algorithms for answering them. Section 4.3 summarizes the results of this chapter.

4.1 Background

A common class of geometric retrieval problems of points in the plane is as follows. Given a set of n points, efficiently report all the points that lie inside a query whose shape is a half-plane [22,60,61], an axis-aligned rectangle [63], a triangle [60,61,64] or a polygon [65].

Numerous solutions for this class of problems have been developed for exact points and exact queries. However, half-plane point retrieval queries in the presence of geometric uncertainty have received significantly less attention. In many situations, the locations of the points and the queries cannot be determined exactly, so modeling their location uncertainty is required to understand the variability of the location of the points with respect to the queries.

The most common approach to model geometric uncertainty is to model point location uncertainty by bounding the point coordinates variability to a region around it. The points are classified into three disjoint sets: ABOVE, BELOW and UNCERT. Points are in ABOVE

(BELOW) iff all instances of the points are above/inside (below/ outside) all instances of the half-plane/rectangle/triangle/polygon query; otherwise, they are in UNCERT. While this approach allows exact geometrical analysis of location uncertainty, it cannot model dependencies between the point location uncertainties induced by the problem specifications and the real-world characteristics of these uncertainties.

Ignoring the dependencies between the geometric uncertainties of entities may result in an incorrect classification of the actual geometric uncertainty. Figure 4.1 illustrates this situation with a simple example. Let the parametric uncertainty model $(q, \bar{q}, \Delta)$ be defined by two parameters $(k = 2)$ and a vector $q = (q_1, q_2)$, where $\Delta_1 = [-1, 1], \Delta_2 = [-1, 1]$. Let $p = (14, 0.5)$ be an exact point and let $l_{uv}(q)$ be an uncertain half-plane query that is defined by uncertain points $u(q), v(q)$, where $\bar{u} = (0, 0)$, $A_u = \begin{pmatrix} 0 & 1 \\ 0 & 0 \end{pmatrix}$, $\bar{v} = (8, 0)$, $A_v = \begin{pmatrix} 0 & 0 \\ 0 & 1 \end{pmatrix}$. In this case, $u(q)$ and $v(q)$ are independent and the envelope of $l_{uv}(q)$, $\partial Z(l_{uv}(q))$ consists of six line segments formed by the intersections of the two diagonal lines and the two parallel lines defined by the uppermost and lowermost points in each interval of $\partial Z(u(q)), \partial Z(v(q))$ (Fig. 4.1(a)). Since point p is inside $Z(l_{uv}(q))$, its location is uncertain: It is above $l_{uv}(q)$ for some choices of $u(q), v(q)$ and below $l_{uv}(q)$ for others.

Assume now that the location uncertainties of $u(q)$ and $v(q)$ are dependent, so that when the location of $u(q)$ changes, the location of $v(q)$ changes in the same direction and at the same rate, i.e., $A_u = A_v = \begin{pmatrix} 0 & 1 \\ 0 & 0 \end{pmatrix}$. In this case, $\partial Z(l_{uv}(q))$ consists of two parallel lines (Fig. 4.1(b)). Point p is now always outside $Z(l_{uv}(q))$ and thus always above line $l_{uv}(q)$. Consequently, point p will be above $l_{uv}(q)$ regardless of the location uncertainty of $l_{uv}(q)$. Ignoring the dependency between $u(q)$ and $v(q)$ leads to an incorrect classification of p.

Numerous geometric retrieval algorithms for exact points and shapes have been developed. Agarwal and Ericson [63] present an ample survey of the known techniques and data structures for range searching and their application to related geometric search problems. Edelsbrunner and Welzl [66] describe an $O(n^{\log 2(1+\sqrt{5})-1})$ time algorithm for half-plane retrieval queries with an $O(n)$ space data

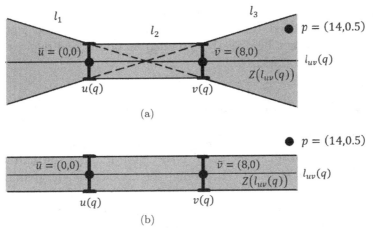

Fig. 4.1. Example that illustrates that ignoring the dependency of two uncertain points $u(q)$ and $v(q)$ leads to an incorrect classification. Let $p = (14, 0.5)$ be an exact point (black dot) and $l_{uv}(q)$ be an uncertain half-plane query defined by uncertain points $u(q)$ and $v(q)$, where $\bar{u} = (0,0), \bar{v} = (8,0)$ (black dots). The location uncertainty of $u(q)$ and $v(q)$ lies in vertical intervals of length 2 units (thick black segments). The location uncertainty of line $l_{uv}(q)$ is the region $Z(l_{uv}(q))$; (a) point uncertainties are independent, the envelope of $Z(l_{uv}(q))$ consists of six line segments: l_1, l_2, l_3 and their mirror segments at the bottom envelope. Point p is above $l_{uv}(q)$ for some instances of $u(q)$ and $v(q)$, and below $l_{uv}(q)$ for others; (b) when the point uncertainties are dependent, so that the locations of $u(q)$ and $v(q)$ change in the same direction and at the same rate, the envelope of $Z(l_{uv}(q))$ consists of two parallel lines. In this case, point p is always above line $l_{uv}(q)$.

structure for storing the points. Chazelle *et al.* [60] describe an optimal $O(\log n + m)$ time and $O(n^2)$ space algorithm to solve this problem based on duality. Welzl [64] and Cole and Yap [61] study the problem of point retrieval inside a triangle query and present $O(\sqrt{n} \log^3 n)$ and $O(\log n \log \log n)$ query time algorithms with $O(n)$ and $O(n^2 / \log n)$ space data structures for storing the points, respectively. Willard [65] studies the problem of point retrieval inside a polygon defined by a constant number of line segments and describes an $O(n^{\log_6 4})$ time retrieval algorithm with $O(n)$ space complexity. Chazelle and Edelsbrunner [67] study the problem of preprocessing a set of n points to efficiently answer convex shape queries and describe an optimal $O(m + \log n)$ time algorithm where m is the number of output points, assuming that the test of a single point inside the convex shape takes $O(1)$ time. The drawback of this algorithm is that the query shape is fixed. The main disadvantage of all these methods is that they cannot be directly extended to points and queries with geometric uncertainties.

4.2   Half-Plane Point Retrieval Queries

We define a family of half-plane point retrieval queries as follows (Fig. 4.2). Given an exact or LPGUM line defining the half-plane query and an exact or LPGUM point set, we classify the points into three disjoint sets: ABOVE, BELOW and UNCERT. Points are in ABOVE (BELOW) iff all instances of the points are above (below) all instances of the query line; otherwise, they are in UNCERT. We distinguish between one-shot and recurrent half-plane queries.

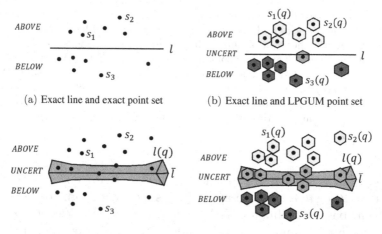

(a) Exact line and exact point set   (b) Exact line and LPGUM point set

(c) LPGUM line and exact point set   (d) LPGUM line and LPGUM point set

Fig. 4.2.   Illustrations of half-plane point retrieval queries; (a) exact line l and exact point set S; (b) exact line l and LPGUM point set. The light gray points are in the subset ABOVE, the dark gray points are in the subset BELOW, and the remaining points are in the subset UNCERT; (c) LPGUM line $l(q)$ and exact point set — the points that are above $l(q)$ are in the subset ABOVE, the points that are below $l(q)$ are in the subset BELOW, the points that intersect $l(q)$ are in the subset UNCERT; (d) LPGUM line $l(q)$ and LPGUM point set — the light gray points are in the subset ABOVE, the dark gray points are in the subset BELOW, the remaining points are in the subset UNCERT.

4.2.1 Exact line and exact points

Let $S = \{s_1, \ldots, s_n\}$ be a set of n exact points and let l be an exact line. For one-shot half-plane queries, the points are directly classified with respect to a half-plane query line into two mutually exclusive sets ABOVE(S, l) and BELOW(S, l) in $O(n)$ time.

Chazelle *et al.* [60] describe an optimal $O(\log n + m)$ algorithm for recurrent queries, where $m = |\text{BELOW}(S, l)|$ is the number of points that are below exact line l. The algorithm requires $O(n)$ space and $O(n \log n)$ preprocessing time.

4.2.2 Exact line and LPGUM points

Let $S(q) = \{s_1(q), \ldots, s_n(q)\}$ be a set of n LPGUM independent or dependent points and let l be an exact line. The points in $S(q)$ are classified with respect to the line into three mutually exclusive sets: ABOVE$(S(q), l)$ and BELOW$(S(q), l)$, the subsets of points of $S(q)$ that are always above/below line $l, \forall q_a \in \Delta$, and UNCERT$(S(q), l)$, the subset of points of $S(q)$ such that $\exists q_a, q_b \in \Delta, \exists s_i(q) \in S(q)$ so that $s_i(q_a)$ is above l and $s_i(q_b)$ is below l.

Given a point set $S(q)$ and an exact line l, the one-shot half-plane point query is computed by first constructing the zonotope of the LPGUM points in $O(nk \log k)$. Then, for each vertex that defines an envelope of a zonotope of $s_i(q)$, we test if it is above or below line l. When all the vertices of the envelope of $s_i(q)$ are above (below) line l, then $s_i(q) \in$ ABOVE$(S(q), l)$ ($s_i(q) \in$ BELOW$(S(q), l)$). When some of the vertices of the envelope of $s_i(q)$ are above line l and others are below it, $s_i(q) \in$ UNCERT$(S(q), l)$. The time complexity of testing each point is $O(k)$ and $O(nk)$ for all points. Thus, the time complexity of a single one-shot half-plane query is $O(nk \log k)$.

For recurrent half-plane point queries, we use the same method as for the exact point set (Section 4.2.1). It consists of two steps: (1) construct the zonotope of the LPGUM points in $O(nk \log k)$ time; (2) for each point $s_i(q)$, process each vertex that defines the envelope of point $s_i(q)$ as an exact point [60]. Overall, the construction time is $O(nk \log nk)$ with $O(nk)$ space.

The query inputs an exact line l and reports the point $s_i(q) \in S(q)$ in the primal plane for which some of its vertices are below (above) line l and the others are not. This takes $O(mk)$ time, where m is the number of points that are below (above) exact line l, $m =$ $|\text{BELOW}(S(q),l)| + |\text{UNCERT}(S(q),l)|$ ($m = |\text{ABOVE}(S(q),l)| +$ $|\text{UNCERT}(S(q),l)|$). The query time complexity is thus $O(\log nk + mk)$.

Correctness: The uncertainty zone of an LPGUM point $s_i(q)$ is defined by a zonotope. When all the vertices of the zonotope are above or below the exact line l, then $\forall q_a \in \Delta$, point instance $s_i(q_a)$ is above or below l. When l intersects the uncertainty zone of LPGUM point $s_i(q)$, then by the convexity of the zonotope, some of the vertices of the zonotope will be above l while the other are below l. In this case, $\exists q_a, q_b \in \Delta$ such that $s_i(q_a)$ is above l and $s_i(q_b)$ is below l.

4.2.3   LPGUM line and exact points

Let S be a set of n points and let $l(q)$ be an independent or dependent LPGUM line. The points in S are classified in $O(k^2 + n \log k)$ time with respect to $l(q)$ into three mutually exclusive sets: $\text{ABOVE}(S, l(q))$ and $\text{BELOW}(S, l(q))$, the subsets of points of S that are always above/below line $l(q)$, $\forall q_a \in \Delta$, and $\text{UNCERT}(S, l(q))$, the subset of points of S such that $\exists q_a, q_b \in \Delta$, $\exists s_i \in S$ so that s_i is above $l(q_a)$ and s_i is below $l(q_b)$.

Given a point set S and an LPGUM line $l(q)$, the one-shot half-plane query is computed by first computing the LPGUM line envelope in $O(k^2)$ as described in Section 3.2.3. Then, for each exact point $s_i \in S$, we test if it is above (below) two monotonic chains that define the LPGUM line envelope, and if so $s_i \in \text{ABOVE}(S, l(q))$ ($s_i \in \text{BELOW}(S, l(q))$). When a point s_i is below the upper envelope of $l(q)$ and above the lower envelope of $l(q)$, then $s_i \in \text{UNCERT}(S, l(q))$. Since each chain has $O(k)$ monotonic segments, the complexity of testing each point is $O(\log k)$ and $O(n \log k)$ time for all points. Thus, the time complexity of a one-shot half-plane query is $O(k^2 + n \log k)$.

For recurrent half-plane point queries, we describe next a method based on the triangle query retrieval method of Cole and Yap [61]. In this method, the points are stored in an $O(n^2/\log n)$ data structure computed in $O(n^2 \log n)$ time. A triangle query takes $O(\log n \log \log n)$ time.

This method requires approximating the parabola segments of the LPGUM line query envelopes with line segments. The required

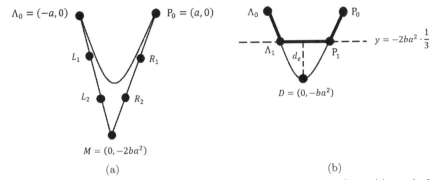

Fig. 4.3. Illustration of the approximation of a parabola $y = (x - a)(x + a) \cdot b$ for $r = 3$; (a) two line segments tangent to the parabola at points $\Lambda_0 = (-a, 0)$ and $P_0 = (a, 0)$ (black points). They intersect at point $M = (0, -2ba^2)$. Both tangents divided into three equal parts each at points $\Lambda_0, L_1 = \left(-\frac{a}{3}, -\frac{2ba^2}{3}\right), L_2 = \left(-\frac{2a}{3}, -\frac{4ba^2}{3}\right), M$ and $P_0, R_1 = \left(\frac{a}{3}, -\frac{2ba^2}{3}\right), R_2 = \left(\frac{2a}{3}, -\frac{4ba^2}{3}\right)$ (black points); (b) three line segments that approximate the parabola. The maximum approximation error occurs at distance d_ε (dotted line segment) between the extreme point of the parabola, $D = (0, -ba^2)$, and the segment define by endpoints Λ_1 and P_1. The equation of the supporting line of this segment is $y = -2ba^2 \cdot \frac{1}{3}$ (dotted line).

number of line segments for each parabola segments is a function of an approximation error denoted by ε, $0 < \varepsilon \leq 1$.

We describe first the parabola segment approximation method (Fig. 4.3). Assume without loss of generality that the parabola segment is symmetric along the y axis and has the form $y = (x - a)(x + a) \cdot b$. We approximate the parabola with r segments computed as follows.

Assume without loss of generality that r is odd. Start with computing the $r + 1$ points on the parabola at $\lceil r/2 \rceil$ elevation lines $0, -\frac{2ba^2}{r}, -\frac{4ba^2}{r}, \cdots, -\frac{2(\lceil r/2 \rceil - 1)ba^2}{r}$; denote those points by $\Lambda_0, \ldots, \Lambda_{\lceil r/2 \rceil - 1}$ and $P_0, \ldots, P_{\lceil r/2 \rceil - 1}$ corresponding to the left and right side of the parabola. We create the approximation segments by defining their endpoints at Λ_0 and Λ_1, followed by Λ_1 and Λ_2 and so on up to $\Lambda_{\lceil r/2 \rceil - 1}$ and $P_{\lceil r/2 \rceil - 1}$, and then to $P_{\lceil r/2 \rceil - 1}$ and $P_{\lceil r/2 \rceil - 2}$ down to the line segment defined by P_1 and P_0.

By the parabola convexity, the maximum approximation error occurs for distance d_ε between the extreme point of the parabola, $D = (0, -ba^2)$, and the line segment defined by $\Lambda_{\lceil r/2 \rceil - 1}$ and $P_{\lceil r/2 \rceil - 1}$.

The equation of the line segment supporting line is $y = -2ba^2 \cdot \frac{r-1}{2r}$. That is,

$$0 \le d_\varepsilon = ba^2 - \frac{ba^2(r-1)}{r}$$

First, note that $ba^2 \ge 0$ is a constant. Second, when $d_\varepsilon = \frac{ba^2}{r} \le \varepsilon$, $r \ge O(1/\varepsilon)$. Therefore, for an approximation error $< \varepsilon$, $O(1/\varepsilon)$ line segments suffice to approximate the parabolic segments.

The intuition behind this approximation is the existence of two line segments tangent to the parabola at points $\Lambda_0 = (-a, 0)$, $P_0 = (a, 0)$ that intersect at point $M = (0, -2ba^2)$. Each line segment is divided into r equal segments at points $L_1 = \left(-\frac{a}{r}, -\frac{2ba^2}{r}\right), \ldots, L_{r-1} = \left(-\frac{a(r-1)}{r}, -\frac{2(r-1)ba^2}{r}\right)$ and at points $R_1 = \left(\frac{a}{r}, -\frac{2ba^2}{r}\right), \ldots, R_{r-1} = \left(\frac{a(r-1)}{r}, -\frac{2(r-1)ba^2}{r}\right)$, respectively.

We preprocess the exact points to compute triangle queries as follows [61]. The query algorithm consists of five steps: (1) Construct the LPGUM line envelope; (2) divide the plane into $O(k)$ vertical slabs defined by the $O(k)$ chain endpoints (Fig. 4.4(a)) and the leftmost and rightmost points; (3) replace each parabola segment of the line envelope with $O(1/\varepsilon)$ line segments defined by the endpoints of the parabola segment; (4) triangulate each interval defined by two adjacent slabs bounded by the upper and lower envelope of the LPGUM line (Fig. 4.4(b)), thereby obtaining $O(k/\varepsilon)$ triangles; (5) answer $O(k/\varepsilon)$ triangle queries and report all the points that are inside the line envelope. For triangles that originate from a parabola segment, compute queries for the points that are inside the parabola segment.

The time complexity of the query is $O(k^2 + (k \log n \log \log n)/\varepsilon + m)$: The first step takes $O(k^2)$ time; steps 2–4 take $O(k/\varepsilon)$ time. The fifth step takes $O((k \log n \log \log n)/\varepsilon + m)$ where $m = |\text{UNCERT}(S, l(q))|$ plus all the points placed between the parabola segment and the line segments which approximate the parabola segment in step 3. The computation requires $O(k)$ space for storing the LPGUM line, $O(n^2/\log n)$ space for storing n exact points and $O(k/\varepsilon)$ space for storing $O(k/\varepsilon)$ triangles. Thus, the overall space complexity is $O(n^2/\log n + k/\varepsilon)$.

An alternative method for the triangle query retrieval is the method of Welzl [64]. In this method, the points are stored in an $O(n)$ data structure computed in $O(n \log n)$ time; a triangle query

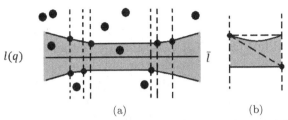

Fig. 4.4. Illustration of LPGUM line query and exact point set: (a) a horizontal LPGUM line $l(q)$ and an exact point set S (large black dots); the upper and lower envelopes of $l(q)$ (solid lines) are divided by k vertical slabs (dotted lines) at the chain segment endpoint (small black dots); (b) splitting of an interval defined by two adjacent vertical slabs and the upper and lower envelope of the LPGUM line into two triangles; the upper horizontal dotted line segment replaces the parabola segment of a triangle (triangulation for $\varepsilon = 1$).

takes $O(\sqrt{n}\log^3 n)$ time. In our case, the overall complexity is the preprocessing time is $O(n\log n)$, the time complexity of the query is $O(k^2 + (k\sqrt{n}\log^3 n)/\varepsilon + m)$, where $m = |\text{UNCERT}(S, l(q))|$ plus all the points placed between the parabola segment and the line segments which approximate the parabola segment in step 3, and the space complexity is $O(n + k/\varepsilon)$.

4.2.4 LPGUM line and LPGUM points with no mutual dependencies

Let $S(q) = \{s_1(q), \ldots, s_n(q)\}$ be a set of n LPGUM dependent or independent points and let $l(q)$ be an LPGUM line (dependent or independent), such that point set $S(q)$ and line $l(q)$ are independent. The points in $S(q)$ are classified with respect to the line into three mutually exclusive sets: $\text{ABOVE}(S(q), l(q))$ and $\text{BELOW}(S(q), l(q))$ are the subsets of points of $S(q)$ that are always above/below line $l(q), \forall q_a \in \Delta$, and $\text{UNCERT}(S(q), l(q))$ is the subset of points of $S(q)$ such that $\exists q_a, q_b \in \Delta, \exists s_i(q) \in S(q)$ so that $s_i(q_a)$ is above $l(q_a)$ and $s_i(q_b)$ is below $l(q_b)$.

We describe next an $O(k^2 + nk\log k)$ time one-shot half-plane query algorithm. First, we construct the zonotope of the LPGUM point set $S(q)$ in $O(nk\log k)$ and compute the LPGUM line envelope in $O(k^2)$ time. Then, for each vertex that defines an envelope of a zonotope of $s_i(q)$, we test if it is above or below the two monotonic segment chains that define the LPGUM line $l(q)$

envelope. When all the vertices of of $s_i(q)$ are above (below), the two monotonic segment chains, then $s_i(q) \in \text{ABOVE}(S(q), l(q))$ $(s_i(q) \in \text{BELOW}(S(q), l(q)))$. Otherwise, either when a vertex of the envelope of $s_i(q)$ is inside the envelope of line $l(q)$, or any of the vertices of $s_i(q)$ are above and others are below the two monotonic chains, then $s_i(q) \in \text{UNCERT}(S(q), l(q))$. Since the time complexity of testing each point is $O(k \log k)$, it is $O(nk \log k)$ for all points. Thus, one-shot half-plane query time complexity is $O(k^2 + nk \log k)$.

For half-plane queries for a fixed point set $S(q)$ and different LPGUM lines, we use a method based on that of Sections 4.2.2 and 4.2.3. The preprocessing consists of constructing the zonotope of the LPGUM points in $O(nk \log k)$ time and then preprocessing the vertices of the points to efficiently answer triangle queries [61]. In this method, the points are stored in an $O((nk)^2 / \log nk)$ space data structure. The bounding box of the $O(nk)$ vertices is computed and the number of vertices that define each zonotope are stored in a hash table in $O(nk)$ time. The hash table is an array such that cell i contains the sum of vertices of $s_i(q)$. This method requires approximating parabola segments with line segments as described in Section 4.2.3. In this case, the approximation segments should be below the parabolas. The $O(1/\varepsilon)$ line segments needed for approximation depend on the approximation error $0 < \varepsilon \leq 1$.

The recurrent query algorithm consists of three steps: (1) Compute the LPGUM line envelope in $O(k^2)$ time; (2) replace each parabola segment of the upper line envelope with $O(1/\varepsilon)$ line segments defined by the endpoints of the parabola segment to obtain a total of $O(k/\varepsilon)$ line segments; (3) find the intersection of the bounding box and the chain of $O(k/\varepsilon)$ line segments obtained in step 2. There are three possible cases (Fig. 4.5):

1. the bounding box does not intersect the chain and it is placed downward to the chain;
2. the bounding box does not intersect the chain and it is placed upward to the chain;
3. the intersection is convex.

In the first and second cases, all the points are above/below the line, so no point will always will be above/below to the line. In the third

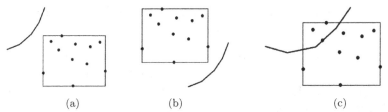

(a)   (b)   (c)

Fig. 4.5.   Illustration of the point set bounding box and the upper envelope of the LPGUM line (a chain): (a and b) cases 1 and 2: bounding box is below (above) the chain and does not intersect it — none of the points will be above (below) the line for every line instance; (c) case 3: bounding box intersects the chain.

case, we perform the following additional steps: (4) Triangulate the convex intersection computed in step 3 to obtain a total of $O(k/\varepsilon)$ triangles; (5) answer the $O(k/\varepsilon)$ triangles queries. For triangles that originated from a parabola segment, compute queries for the vertices that are inside the parabola segment; (6) construct a hash table for each vertex belonging to point $s_i(q)$ computed in step 5 and increase by one the value of cell i; (7) test if the value of the cells computed in step 6 is equal to the number of vertices in the hash table that was constructed in the preprocessing stage. Finally, report all the points for which all their vertices are above the upper line envelope.

The time complexity of the query is $O(k^2+(k\log nk\log\log nk)/\varepsilon+mk)$: Steps 2–4 take $O(k/\varepsilon)$ time; the fifth step takes $O((k\log nk\log\log nk)/\varepsilon + mk)$ [61], where m is the number of points in ABOVE$(S(q),l(q))$ and vertices of the points in $UNCERT(S(q),l(q))$, depending on the approximation error ε; steps 6–7 take $O(mk)$. The space complexity is as follows: $O(k)$ space is required to store the LPGUM line, $O((nk)^2/\log nk)$ space to store nk vertices of n LPGUM points, $O(k/\varepsilon)$ space to store $O(k/\varepsilon)$ triangles and $O(n)$ space to store two hash tables. Overall, the space complexity is $O((nk)^2/\log nk + k/\varepsilon)$.

An alternative method for the triangle query retrieval is the method of Welzl [64]. In this method, the points are stored in an $O(nk)$ data structure computed in $O(nk\log nk)$ time; a triangle query takes $O(\sqrt{nk}\log^3 nk)$ time. Overall, the preprocessing time is $O(nk\log nk)$ and the query time is $O(k^2 + (k\sqrt{n}\log^3 n)/\varepsilon + mk)$, where m is the number of points in ABOVE$(S(q),l(q))$ and vertices of the points in UNCERT$(S(q),l(q))$, where ε is the desired approximation error. The space complexity is $O(nk + k/\varepsilon)$.

4.2.5   Dependent LPGUM line and LPGUM points with dependencies between them

Let $S(q) = \{s_1(q), \ldots, s_n(q)\}$ be a set of n LPGUM dependent or independent points and let $l(q)$ be an LPGUM dependent or independent line, such that point set $S(q)$ and line $l(q)$ are dependent.

For one-shot half-plane queries, the points in $S(q)$ can be classified with respect to the line into the three mutually exclusive sets in $O(nk^2)$ time. For each point, we test in $O(k^2)$ if there is an orientation flip between one of the LPGUM point $s_i(q)$ in the point set $S(q)$ and any two points on the LPGUM line $l(q)$ (Section 3.3.1). Since the line envelope can be computed in $O(k^2)$ time (Section 3.2), the orientation flip test will also take $O(k^2)$ time.

We consider next the recurrent case; we start with a Lemma and then describe the query algorithm.

Lemma 4.1. *When an LPGUM point $s(q)$ is fully contained in the uncertainty zone of an LPGUM line $l(q)$, then $\exists q_a \in \Delta$ such that line $l(q_a)$ is above point $s(q_a)$.*

Proof.   The uncertainty zone of an LPGUM point is a zonotope. The line envelope consists of two monotone segment chains and the two components outside the uncertainty zone of $l(q)$ are both convex (Fig. 4.6(a)). The two convex components can be separated by a line, therefore $\exists q_a \in \Delta$ such that $l(q_a)$ is above the zonotope. Thus, for parameter instance q_a, the point $s(q_a)$ is below the line $l(q_a)$.   □

Consequently, it is sufficient to test only points that intersect the upper envelope of the line (Fig. 4.6(b)). The points that are above the line for every parameter instance due to their coupled dependencies with the line uncertainty are classified to the set $\text{ABOVE}(S(q), l(q))$.

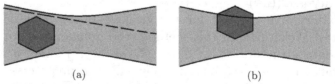

(a)   (b)

Fig. 4.6.   Illustration of LPGUM point (dark gray) and LPGUM line (light gray): (a) the LPGUM point envelope is fully contained in the uncertainty zone of the line; the dotted line is a line instance that is above the zonotope; (b) the LPGUM point envelope intersects the upper envelope of the line.

For the recurrent queries, we use the same algorithm as for the independent case (Section 4.2.4) with an additional test to determine if, when a point envelope intersects the line envelope, the intersection indeed occurs subject to the parameter dependencies: There is no intersection between line $l(q)$ and point $s_i(q)$ iff there is no orientation flip between point $s_i(q)$ and any two points on the line $l(q)$.

We first run the algorithm in Section 4.2.4 and then test for orientation flips (Section 3.3.1) for the subset of points that intersect the line envelope. The result is the set of LPGUM points whose number of vertices that are above the line is not equal to the number of vertices in the hash table that was constructed in the preprocessing stage. The additional test takes $O(k^2)$ time. Thus, the overall time complexity is $O(mk^2 + (k \log nk \log \log nk)/\varepsilon)$, where mk is the number of vertices in ABOVE$(S(q), l(q))$ and a subset of the points in UNCERT$(S(q), l(q))$, depending on the approximation error ε.

Note that when $m = O(n)$, the complexity can be improved by using the one-shot half-plane query algorithm whose time complexity is $O(nk^2)$.

As an alternative, we can use the method of Welzl [64]. The overall time complexity then is $O(mk^2 + (k \log nk \log \log nk)/\varepsilon)$.

4.3   Summary

We have defined a family of geometric half-plane retrieval queries of points in the plane in the presence of geometric uncertainty in the LPGUM model and have described efficient algorithms to answer the queries. The problems include exact and uncertain point sets and half-plane queries defined by an exact or uncertain line whose location uncertainties are independent or dependent and are defined by k real valued parameters. We classify the points into three disjoint sets: ABOVE, BELOW and UNCERT. We describe algorithms for one-shot and for recurrent half-plane queries. The algorithms rely on a new efficient $O(k^2)$ time and space algorithm for computing the envelope of the LPGUM line that defines the half-plane query. Table 4.1 summarizes the time and space complexity of the half-plane retrieval queries.

Table 4.1. Summary of the time and space complexity of the half-plane point retrieval queries for an exact or uncertain line and n exact or uncertain points, where m is the number of output points for one-shot and recurrent half-plane queries and $0 < \varepsilon \leq 1$ is the approximation error.

Line	Points	One-shot query (time)	Recurrent queries	
			Preprocessing (time\space)	Recurrent query (time)
Exact	Exact	$O(n)$	$O(n \log n)$ $O(n)$	$O(\log n + m)$
	Uncertain	$O(nk \log k)$	$O(nk \log nk)$ $O(nk)$	$O(\log nk + mk)$
Uncertain	Exact	$O(k^2 + n \log k)$	$O(n^2 \log n)$ $O(n^2 \log n + k/\varepsilon)$	$O(k^2 + (k \log n \log \log n)/\varepsilon + m)$
	Uncertain Independent	$O(k^2 + nk \log k)$	$O((nk)^2 \log nk)$ $O((nk)^2/\log nk + k/\varepsilon)$	$O(k^2 + (k \log nk \log \log nk)/\varepsilon + m)$
	Uncertain Dependent	$O(nk^2)$	$O((nk)^2 \log nk)$ $O((nk)^2/\log nk + k/\varepsilon)$	$O(mk^2 + (k \log nk \log \log nk)/\varepsilon)$

Line	Points	Recurrent queries	
		Preprocessing (time\space)	Recurrent query (time)
Uncertain	Exact	$O(n \log n)$ $O(n + k/\varepsilon)$	$O(k^2 + (k\sqrt{n} \log^3 n)/\varepsilon + m)$
	Uncertain Independent	$O(nk \log nk)$ $O(nk + k/\varepsilon)$	$O(k^2 + (k\sqrt{n} \log^3 n)/\varepsilon + k)$
	Uncertain Dependent	$O(nk \log nk)$ $O(nk + k/\varepsilon)$	$O(mk^2 + (k \log nk \log \log nk)/\varepsilon)$

Top table: the first two columns indicate the line and point set certainty. The third column lists the time complexity of a one-shot half-point query. The fourth and fifth columns list the preprocessing time and space complexity and the query time complexity of a recurrent query. The results for the uncertain line recurrent query are based on the method of Cole and Yap [61]; Bottom table: the third and fourth columns list the preprocessing time, space complexity and the query time complexity of a recurrent query based on the method of Welzl [64].

Chapter 5

Euclidean Minimum Spanning Trees

This chapter addresses the problems of constructing the Euclidean minimum spanning tree (EMST) of points in the plane with mutually dependent location uncertainties, testing its stability and computing its total weight. Section 5.1 introduces the problem and reviews the relevant literature. Section 5.2 defines the uncertain EMST of a set of LPGUM points and its properties. Section 5.3 presents algorithms for comparison of uncertain Euclidean graph edge weights. Section 5.4 describes algorithms for testing the stability of an uncertain EMST. Section 5.5 describes a method for computing the minimum and maximum weight of a stable uncertain EMST. Section 5.6 summarizes this chapter.

5.1 Background

A variety of models and representations have been proposed to model Euclidean minimum spanning tree (EMST) of a set of points in the plane in the presence of geometric uncertainty. Both deterministic and probabilistic approaches have been proposed.

A key limitation of nearly all existing geometric uncertainty models is that they ignore the possible coupling between edges weights, which precludes their use for EMST construction with uncertain points because the graph weights are always coupled: The EMST of three uncertain points s_1, s_2, s_3 depends on their pairwise distances $(s_1, s_2), (s_2, s_3), (s_3, s_1)$, which are coupled because they share a common point s_1.

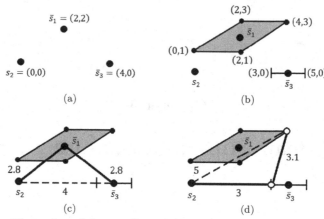

Fig. 5.1.   Illustration of the coupling of the graph weights of an EMST of three uncertain points that cause EMST instability: (a) exact point $s_2 = (0,0)$ and uncertain points s_1 and s_3 whose nominal locations are $\bar{s}_1 = (2,2), \bar{s}_3 = (4,0)$ (black dots); (b) the location uncertainty of point s_3 is a line interval whose vertices are $(3,0)$ and $(5,0)$ (thin black lines); the location uncertainty of point s_3 is a convex polygon whose vertices are $\langle(2,3),(0,1),(2,1),(4,3)\rangle$ (small black dots, thin black lines); the polygon interior (gray) shows the possible point locations; (c) EMST edges (thick black lines) and distances (black and dotted lines) of the nominal point instances $s_1 = (2,2)$ and $s_3 = (4,0)$; (d) EMST edges and distances of the point instances $s_1 = (4,3)$ and $s_3 = (3,0)$ (white dots). The edge distances $s_1 s_2$ and $s_2 s_3$ are coupled and yield two different EMSTs.

Figure 5.1 illustrates this situation. Let the parametric uncertainty model $(q,\bar{q},\Delta)$ be defined by two parameters $(k = 2)$ and a vector $q = (q_1,q_2)$, where $\Delta_1 = [-1,1], \Delta_2 = [-0.5,-0.5]$. Let $s_2 = (0,0)$ be an exact point and let $s_1(q)$ and $s_3(q)$ be two uncertain points whose nominal locations are $\bar{s}_1 = (2,2)$ and $\bar{s}_3 = (4,0)$ (Fig. 5.1(a)). Let the sensitivity matrix of point $s_3(q)$ be $A_3 = \begin{pmatrix} -1 & 0 \\ 0 & 0 \end{pmatrix}$, i.e., the possible point instances lie in a horizontal interval of length 2 units whose vertices are $(3,0)$ and $(5,0)$ (Fig. 5.1(b)). Let the sensitivity matrix of point $s_1(q)$ be $A_1 = \begin{pmatrix} 1 & 0 \\ 2 & 2 \end{pmatrix}$, i.e., a convex polygon defined by its vertices $\langle(2,3),(0,1),(2,1),(4,3)\rangle$ (Fig. 5.1(b)).

Consider now the following two scenarios (Fig. 5.1(c) and (d)). For the nominal point instances $\bar{s}_1 = (2,2)$ and $\bar{s}_3 = (4,0)$ (Fig. 5.1(c)), the pairwise distances are $s_1 s_2 = \sqrt{8} \approx 2.8$, $s_1 s_3 = \sqrt{8} \approx 2.8$ and $s_2 s_3 = 4$, so the EMST consists of edges $s_1 s_2$ and $s_1 s_3$ and its weight is 5.6. For parameter vector instance $q_a = (1,0.5)$, the point instances are $s_1(q_a) = (4, 3)$ and $s_3(q_a) = (3, 0)$, the pairwise point distances are $s_1 s_2 = 5$, $s_1 s_3 = \sqrt{10} \approx 3.1$ and $s_2 s_3 = 3$, so the EMST consists of edges $s_1 s_3$ and $s_2 s_3$ and its weight is 6.1.

Note that the edge distances $s_1 s_2$ and $s_1 s_3$ are coupled because they share common point $s_1(q)$ whose location is uncertain. Moreover, note that there are two EMSTs with different edges depending on the location of uncertain points $s_1(q)$ and $s_3(q)$, so the EMST of uncertain point set $\{s_1(q), s_2, s_3(q)\}$ is topologically unstable.

The topological stability of EMST and related structures of uncertain points has been widely studied. Most works on stability focus on small point location perturbations, e.g., floating point errors and small deviations [34,35]. All these works assume that the point location uncertainties are small, isotropic and independent. None model stability in the presence of dependencies. A geometric model that accounts for dependencies between point locations are kinetic models and their data structures. In a kinetic model, the point locations are time dependent, i.e. points move with a pre-defined speed and trajectory, so their location is known at all times. The key drawback of using kinetic data structures to model location dependencies is that the point location uncertainties all depend on a single common parameter, time. Independent, partially dependent and dependent uncertainties with more parameters cannot be accounted for in this model.

Finding the maximum weight bounds for unstable EMST with point location uncertainties modeled as disjoint independent rectangles/circles, also referred to as the minimum spanning tree with neighborhoods (MSTN) problem, has been shown to be NP-hard [68–70]. Thus, EMST stability testing is required prior to computing its weight bounds. In this context, the sensitivity and variability of the EMST with respect to point locations has also been researched. Agarwal *et al.* present a method for computing an MST whose edge weights are linear functions of a single parameter [71]. However, the important case of multi-parameter dependent point location uncertainty has not been addressed.

5.2 Uncertain EMST: Definitions and Properties

We define next the uncertain EMST of a set of LPGUM points and its properties.

Definition 5.1. *The **uncertain Euclidean graph** of an LPGUM point set $S(q) = \{s_1(q), \ldots, s_n(q)\}$ defined by n sensitivity matrices, each of size $k \times 2$ sensitivity matrices $A_1, \ldots, A_n$ over parametric uncertainty model $(q, \bar{q}, \Delta)$ is an undirected weighted graph:*

$$G(S(q)) = (V(S(q)), E(S(q)))$$

where $V(S(q)) = \{s_i(q)\}$ is the set of vertices corresponding to the LPGUM points $s_i(q)$ and $E(S(q))$ is the set of edges between all pairs of vertices $E(S(q)) = \{e_{ij}(q) = (s_i(q), s_j(q)), \ i \neq j\}$.

The **nominal Euclidean graph** is $\bar{G} = (V(\bar{S}), E(\bar{S}))$ also denoted by $\bar{G} = (\bar{V}, \bar{E})$, where $\bar{V} = \{\bar{s}_i\}$ is the nominal vertex set and $\bar{E} = \{\bar{e}_{ij} = (\bar{s}_i, \bar{s}_j), \ i \neq j\}$ is the nominal edge set.

For example, the point set $S(q) = \{s_1(q), s_2, s_3(q)\}$ in Fig. 5.1(a) has nominal vertex set $\bar{V} = \{\bar{s}_1, s_2, \bar{s}_3\}$.

An **uncertain Euclidean graph** instance of a given parameters instance $q_a \in \Delta$ is the undirected weighted graph $G(S(q_a)) = (V(S(q_a)), E(S(q_a)))$ of point set instance $S(q_a)$. An uncertain Euclidean graph of LPGUM point set is said to be **dependent** iff at least two coordinates of two or more LPGUM points depend on at least one common parameter. Otherwise, the uncertain Euclidean graph is **independent**.

For example, in Fig. 5.1(d), for parameter vector instance $q_a = (1, 0.5)$, the vertices of the weighted graph instance are $V(S(q_a)) = \{(4, 3), (0, 0), (3, 0)\}$. Notice that coordinate x of points $s_1(q)$ and $s_3(q)$ depends on parameter q_1. Therefore, the uncertain Euclidean graph is dependent.

Definition 5.2. *The **uncertain distance** between two LPGUM points $s_i(q), s_j(q)$ is defined by the interval*

$$\text{dist}(s_i(q), s_j(q)) = [\min\_\text{dist}(s_i(q), s_j(q)), \max\_\text{dist}(s_i(q), s_j(q))]$$

where

$$\min\_\text{dist}(s_i(q), s_j(q)) = \min_{q_a \in \Delta} \|s_i(q_a) - s_j(q_a)\|$$

$$\max\_\text{dist}(s_i(q), s_j(q)) = \max_{q_a \in \Delta} \|s_i(q_a) - s_j(q_a)\|$$

The nominal distance between two LPGUM points is the Euclidean distance between their nominal points, $\text{dist}(\bar{s}_i, \bar{s}_j) = \|\bar{s}_i - \bar{s}_j\|$.

For example, in Fig. 5.1(b), $\text{dist}(s_1(q), s_2) = [1, 5]$ and $\text{dist}(\bar{s}_1, s_2) = \sqrt{8} \approx 2.8$.

Definition 5.3. *The **weight** of edge $e_{ij}(q) = (s_i(q), s_j(q))$ is the uncertain distance between its endpoints:*

$$w(e_{ij}(q)) = \text{dist}(s_i(q), s_j(q))$$

The nominal edge $\bar{e}_{ij} = (\bar{s}_i, \bar{s}_j)$ of the nominal Euclidean graph is the edge corresponding to nominal points $\bar{s}_i, \bar{s}_j$ whose weight is $w(e_{ij}(\bar{q})) = w(\bar{e}_{ij}) = \|\bar{s}_i - \bar{s}_j\|$. The edge instance $e_{ij}(q_a) = (s_i(q_a), s_j(q_a))$ for a given parameter instance $q_a \in \Delta$ is the edge corresponding to points $s_i(q_a), s_j(q_a)$ whose weight is $w(e_{ij}(q_a)) = \|s_i(q_a) - s_j(q_a)\|$.

For example, in Fig. 5.1(d), for parameter vector instance $q_a = (1, 0.5)$, $w(e_{12}(q_a)) = \text{dist}(s_1(q_a), s_2) = 5$.

Definition 5.4. *Let $e_{ij}(q) = (s_i(q), s_j(q)), e_{lm}(q) = (s_l(q), s_m(q))$ be two edges of an uncertain Euclidean graph of an LPGUM point set. Edge $e_{lm}(q)$ is said to be **heavier** than edge $e_{ij}(q)$ iff its weight is larger for all parameter instances of q:*

$$w(e_{ij}(q_a)) < w(e_{lm}(q_a)), \forall q_a \in \Delta$$

For example, in Fig. 5.1(b), $w(e_{23}(q)) = [3, 5]$ and $w(e_{12}(q)) = [1, 5]$. Therefore, edge $e_{23}(q)$ is not heavier than edge $e_{12}(q)$ and edge $e_{12}(q)$ is not heavier than edge $e_{23}(q)$.

Definition 5.5. *An **uncertain EMST** of the uncertain Euclidean graph $G(S(q)) = (V(S(q)), E(S(q)))$:*

$$\text{EMST}(S(q)) = (V(S(q)), T(q))$$

where $T(q) \subset E(S(q)), |T(q)| = n - 1$, $\text{EMST}(S(q))$ is a connected graph such that for all parameter instances $q_a \in \Delta$ the sum of the edge weights is smallest, e.g., $\min\{\sum_{e_{ij}(q_a) \in T(q_a)} w(e_{ij}(q_a))\}$.

The nominal EMST is $\text{EMST}(\bar{S}) = (V(\bar{S}), \bar{T})$, also denoted by $\overline{\text{EMST}} = (\bar{V}, \bar{T})$. The EMST instance of a given parameter instance $q_a \in \Delta$ is the Euclidean minimum spanning tree $\text{EMST}(S(q_a)) = (V(S(q_a)), T(q_a))$.

Definition   5.6. *Two   EMST   instances* $\text{EMST}(S(q_a))$ *and* $\text{EMST}(S(q_b))$ *are   said   to   **be   equivalent**,* $\text{EMST}(S(q_a))$ $\equiv$ $\text{EMST}(S(q_b))$,   *iff for each* $e_{ij}(q_a) \in T(q_a)$ *defined by the two point instances* $s_i(q_a), s_j(q_a) \in S(q_a)$ *there is a corresponding edge instance* $e_{ij}(q_b) \in T(q_b)$ *defined by two point instances* $s_i(q_b), s_j(q_b) \in S(q_b)$.

In Fig. 5.1(d), for parameter vector instance $q_a = (1, 0.5)$, the $\text{EMST}(S(q_a)) = (V(S(q_a)), T(q_a))$ where $V(S(q_a)) = \{(4,4), (0,0),$ $(3,0)\}$ so that $T(q_a) = \{e_{13}(q_a), e_{23}(q_a)\}$ and in Fig. 5.1(c), $\overline{\text{EMST}} = (\bar{V}, \bar{T})$ where $\bar{V} = \{(2,2), (0,0), (4,0)\}$ and $\bar{T} = \{\bar{e}_{13}, \bar{e}_{12}\}$. Notice that $e_{23}(q_a) \in T(q_a)$, but $\bar{e}_{23} \notin \bar{T}$, therefore $\text{EMST}(S(q_a)) \neq \overline{\text{EMST}}$.

Definition 5.7. *An uncertain Euclidean minimum spanning tree* $\text{EMST}(S(q))$ *is **stable** iff for every parameter instance* $q_a \in \Delta$, *all EMST instances* $\text{EMST}(S(q_a))$ *are equivalent to the nominal Euclidean minimum spanning tree* $\text{EMST}(\bar{S})$:

$$\text{EMST}(S(q)) = \text{EMST}(\bar{S}), \quad \forall q_a \in \Delta$$

In Fig. 5.1(c and d), $\text{EMST}(S(q))$ is unstable because it has two different instances: the nominal one and one for parameter vector instance $q_a = (1, 0.5)$.

We show next that when an uncertain EMST is unstable, it may have an exponential number of non-equivalent minimum spanning tree instances. This is an undesirable situation, since queries and computations on an unstable uncertain EMST will require exponential time.

Theorem 5.1. *When uncertain Euclidean minimum spanning tree* $\text{EMST}(S(q))$ *is not stable, there may be an exponential number of non-equivalent EMST instances.*

Proof.   By construction of an example that has an exponential number of non-equivalent EMST instances (Fig. 5.2), let $S(q) = \{s_1 \cdot s_2(q), s_3, s_4, s_5(q), s_6, s_7, s_8(q), \ldots, s_{n-3}, s_{n-2}(q), s_{n-1}, s_n\}$ be a set of points and LPGUM points whose locations are arranged as shown in Fig. 5.2(a). Let $m = (n-1)/3$ and $j = (i+1)/3$. For each LPGUM point $s_j(q)$, we define the uncertainty domain $\Delta_j = [-0.1, 0.1]$ and an $m \times 2$ sensitivity matrix $A_j^t = \begin{pmatrix} 0 \cdots 0 & 0 & 0 \cdots 0 \\ 0 \cdots 0 & 1 & 0 \cdots 0 \end{pmatrix}$ such that all the rows are zero except for the row $(A_j)_{j,*} = (0, 1)$

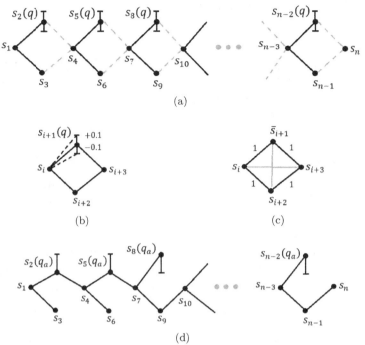

Fig. 5.2.   Illustration of the construction of an uncertain EMST defined on a set of n LPGUM points $S(q) = \{s_1, s_2(q), s_3, s_4, s_5(q), s_6, s_7, s_8(q), \ldots, s_{n-3}, s_{n-2}(q), s_{n-1}, s_n\}$: (a) point locations, uncertainty zone (vertical interval, solid black line), edges that belong to all EMST instances (diagonal solid black lines) and edges that belong to some EMST instances (dotted gray lines); (b) exact points s_i, s_{i+2}, s_{i+3} and LPGUM point $s_{i+1}(q)$ which depends on one parameter, so its uncertainty zone is a vertical line segment that can be in any location in the range of ± 0.1; (c) points s_i, s_{i+2}, s_{i+3} and the nominal point $\bar{s}_{i+1}$. The weight of the black edges is 1. The weight of the gray edges is $2 \cdot \sqrt{0.5}$, each intersects in distance $\sqrt{0.5}$; (d) the EMST$(S(q_a))$.

(Fig. 5.2(b)). Note that the uncertainty domain Δ and the sensitivity matrices $A_1, \ldots, A_m$ are such that $\exists q_\alpha$ for which $\forall s_{i+1}(q_\alpha) \in S(q_\alpha)$, the distance between $s_{i+1}(q_\alpha)$ and s_{i+3} is smaller than the distance between s_{i+2} and s_{i+3}. Also, $\exists q_\beta$ for which $\forall s_{i+1}(q_\beta) \in S(q_\beta)$, the distance between $s_{i+1}(q_\beta)$ and s_{i+3} is larger than the distance between s_{i+2} and s_{i+3}.

We define the nominal point set $\bar{S} = \{s_1 . \bar{s}_2, s_3, s_4, \bar{s}_5, s_6, s_7, \bar{s}_8, \ldots, s_{n-3}, \bar{s}_{n-2}, s_{n-1}, s_n\}$ such that the horizontal and vertical distance between two neighboring points is $2 \cdot \sqrt{0.5} \approx 1.41$. As a result, the edges whose nominal weight is 1 will be part of the EMST (Fig. 5.2(c)).

By construction, each LPGUM point $s_i(q)$ depends only on one parameter $q_j \in q$. Therefore, we can choose any subset of parameters and set them to 0.1 and set the remaining ones to -0.1, so the instances of LPGUM points that depend on the first subset are in the EMST with the lower bottom edges. The LPGUM points that are not in this set define the EMST with the corresponding top edges (Fig. 5.2(d)). Since there are 2^m such subsets, there are 2^m non-equivalent EMSTs.

For the dependent case, we divide the LPGUM points into subsets as follows. Let c be a constant number of LPGUM points in each subset. First, set $c = 2$, and let points $s_2(q), s_5(q)$ depend on parameter q_1. Note that in Fig. 5.2(a) point s_1 is exact, point $s_2(q)$ is an LPGUM point, s_3, s_4 are exact and so on. Points $s_8(q), s_{11}(q)$ depend on parameter q_2 and so on, up to points $s_{n-5}(q), s_{n-2}(q)$ that depend on parameter $q_{m/2}$. Consequently, there are $2^{m/2}$ non-equivalent EMSTs. This will hold for any constant c such that $m/c = \Omega(n)$. $\square$

5.3   Pairwise Uncertain Edge Weight Comparison

The basic element of EMST construction is the comparison of the Euclidean graph edge weights. We describe next two algorithms to determine if one uncertain edge is always heavier than the other: an $O(k \log k)$ geometric algorithm for the independent case and an $O(T(k))$ algebraic algorithm for the dependent case, where $T(k)$ is the time complexity for solving a quadratic optimization problem.

5.3.1   Independent case

We consider two cases: (1) The edges do not share a common point and (2) the edges share a common point (Fig. 5.3).

In the following, we assume that the uncertainty zones of the LPGUM points do not overlap, i.e., that their zonotopes do not intersect. When the uncertainty zones of two LPGUM points overlap, the minimum distance between them is zero, so their uncertain EMST is unstable. Computing the two zonotopes and testing if they

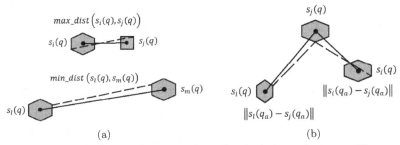

Fig. 5.3. Pairwise edge weight comparisons for the independent case. The uncertainty zones of the LPGUM points appear in gray. The black solid lines show the nominal distance between pairs of points. (a) case 1: two uncertain edges defined by four independent LPGUM points $s_i(q), s_j(q), s_l(q), s_m(q)$. The dashed lines are the maximum and minimum distances between pairs of LPGUM points. (b) case 2: two uncertain edges defined by three LPGUM points $s_i(q), s_j(q), s_l(q)$. The dashed lines correspond to the minimal distance for parameter instance q_a.

intersect can be done in $O(k \log k)$ time and $O(k)$ space for each pair of points [50].

Case 1 (Fig. 5.3(a)): Edges $e_{ij}(q), e_{lm}(q)$ do not share a common LPGUM point. Then, edge $e_{lm}(q)$ is heavier than edge $e_{ij}(q)$ iff the minimum distance between LPGUM points $s_l(q)$ and $s_m(q)$ is larger than the maximum distance between LPGUM point $s_i(q)$ and $s_j(q)$:

$$\text{min \_dist}(s_l(q), s_m(q)) \geq \text{max \_dist}(s_i(q), s_j(q))$$

This test is performed by computing the zonotopes of the points and independently computing the minimum and maximum distances between them in $O(k \log k)$ time and $O(k)$ space.

Case 2 (Fig. 5.3(b)): Edges $e_{ij}(q), e_{jl}(q)$ share a common LPGUM point $s_j(q)$. In this case, the weight of the independent edges $e_{ij}(q), e_{jl}(q)$ depends on point $s_j(q)$. Edge $e_{jl}(q)$ is heavier than edge $e_{ij}(q)$ iff its weight is larger for every parameters instance, i.e., for the parameter instance q_a that minimizes the weight of $e_{jl}(q)$ and maximizes the weight of $e_{ij}(q)$. Thus, $e_{jl}(q)$ is heavier than $e_{ij}(q)$ iff

$$\min_{q \in \Delta}\{\|s_j(q) - s_l(q)\| - \|s_i(q) - s_j(q)\|\} \geq 0$$

Theorem 5.2. *If for an EMST instance, edge $e_{ij}(q)$ is heavier than $e_{jl}(q)$, i.e., $\text{dist}(s_j(q_a), s_l(q_a)) < \text{dist}(s_i(q_a), s_j(q_a))$, then there exist three vertices f, m, c where f (farthest) is a vertex of $Z(s_i(q_a))$, m is* a vertex of $Z(s_j(q_a))$ and c (*closest*) is a vertex of $Z(s_l(q))$ such that they define an EMST instance in which $e_{ij}(q)$ is heavier than $e_{jl}(q)$, i.e., $\text{dist}(m, c) < \text{dist}(m, f)$.

Proof. First, note that the three point instances $s_i(q_a), s_j(q_a)$, $s_l(q_a)$ that minimize the edge weight $\min_{q_a \in \Delta} \{ \| s_j(q) - s_l(q) \| - \| s_i(q) - s_j(q) \| \}$ are on the boundaries of the zonotopes $Z(s_i(q_a)), Z(s_j(q_a)), Z(s_l(q))$. To prove this, we consider the following three cases:

(1) If $s_l(q_a)$ is not on the boundary, it can be moved along $line(s_j(q_a), s_l(q_a))$ to minimize $\| s_j(q) - s_l(q) \|$.
(2) If $s_i(q_a)$ is not on the boundary, it can be moved along the $line(s_i(q_a), s_j(q_a))$ to maximize $\| s_i(q) - s_j(q) \|$.
(3) If $s_j(q_a)$ is not on the boundary, it can in the direction $\vec{v}$ defined as follows. Denote the half-plane defined by the line perpendicular to $line(s_j(q_a), s_l(q_a))$ and passing through $s_j(q_a)$ in the direction decreasing $\| s_j(q) - s_l(q) \|$ by $h(s_j(q_a), s_l(q_a))$, and the half plane defined by the line perpendicular to $line(s_i(q_a), s_j(q_a))$ and passing through $s_j(q_a)$ in the direction increasing $\| s_i(q) - s_j(q) \|$ by $h(s_i(q_a), s_j(q_a))$ (Fig. 5.4). The intersection between the two half-planes and the LPGUM point $s_j(q_a)$ is not empty,

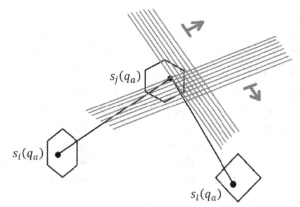

Fig. 5.4.   Illustration of the half-planes defined by the line perpendicular to $line(s_j(q_a), s_l(q_a))$ and passing through $s_j(q_a)$ (dotted gray lines) in the direction decreasing $\| s_j(q) - s_l(q) \|$ (gray arrow) and by the line perpendicular to $line(s_i(q_a), s_j(q_a))$ and passing through $s_j(q_a)$ (dotted gray lines) in the direction increasing $\| s_i(q) - s_j(q) \|$ (gray arrow). Black dots are point instances $s_i(q_a), s_j(q_a), s_l(q_a)$. Gray lines are the intersection $h(s_j(q_a), s_l(q_a)) \cap h(s_j(q_a), s_l(q_a))$.

that is, $h(s_j(q_a), s_l(q_a)) \cap h(s_j(q_a), s_l(q_a)) \cap s_j(q_a) \neq \emptyset$, because $line(s_j(q_a), s_l(q_a))$ and $line(s_i(q_a) - s_j(q_a))$ are not perpendicular. The direction $\vec{v}$ is defined in the intersection $h(s_j(q), s_l(q)) \cap h(s_j(q), s_l(q)) \cap s_j(q_a)$ so that moving $s_j(q_a)$ along $\vec{v}$ minimizes $\|s_j(q) - s_l(q)\|$ and maximizes $\|s_i(q) - s_j(q)\|$.

Moreover, the maximum distance between a point p and a line segment I is always between one of the two endpoints of I; the minimum distance is either the intersection between I and its perpendicular line that passes through p when the intersection is on I or on one of the two endpoints of I (this follows directly from the Pythagorean triangles' theorem).

Therefore, when the minimum distance is the intersection between I and its perpendicular line that passes through p, we can move to one of the endpoints m of I, so that the inequality $\text{dist}(m, c) < \text{dist}(m, f)$ holds. Assume now that $\|c - s_j(q_a)\| = \|f - s_j(q_a)\|$ and rotate $I, c, f, s_j(q_a)$ so that I is perpendicular to the x axis. Consider now the circle defined by the center point $s_j(q_a)$ and the radius $\|c - s_j(q_a)\| = \|f - s_j(q_a)\|$. We distinguish between two cases (Fig. 5.5(a) and (b)):

1. Points c and f are both on the same side of line segment I. Consider the case where f is in the lower half of the circle (Fig. 5.5(a)). Then, moving upward from point $s_j(q_a)$ to the upper endpoint of segment I increases the distances $\|c - s_j(q_a)\|, \|f - s_j(q_a)\|$ so that $\|c - s_j(q_a)\| < \|f - s_j(q_a)\|$ (this follows directly from the inscribed and central angle theorem). The same holds when f is in the upper half of the circle and moves downward.

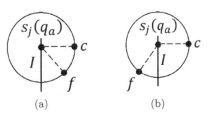

(a)   (b)

Fig. 5.5. Illustration of the circle defined by the center point $s_j(q_a)$ and the radius $\|c - s_j(q_a)\| = \|f - s_j(q_a)\|$ (dotted lines). Points $c, f, s_j(q_a)$ are shown as black points; line segment I is perpendicular to the segments defined by the endpoints c and $s_j(q_a)$. (a) Case 1: points c and f are on the same side of line segment I; (b) Case 2: points c and f are on different sides of line segment I.

2. Points c and f are on different sides of line segment I. First, when line segment defined by the endpoints f and $s_j(q_a)$ is perpendicular to line segment I, moving downward or upward from point $s_j(q_a)$ preserves the distance equality, $\|c - s_j(q_a)\| = \|f - s_j(q_a)\|$. Otherwise, when f is in the lower half of the circle (Fig. 5.5(b)), the angle defined by points $f, s_j(q_a)$ and the lower endpoint of I is $< 90°$. Thus, moving upward to the upper endpoint of segment I increases both distances so that $\|c - s_j(q_a)\| < \|f - s_j(q_a)\|$ (this also follows directly from the inscribed and central angle theorem). The same holds when f is in the upper half of the circle and moves downward.

□

Table 5.1 lists an $O(k \log k)$ time algorithm for testing whether edge $e_{jl}(q)$ is heavier than edge $e_{ij}(q)$.

Theorem 5.3. *The algorithm listed in Table* 5.1 *for comparing the weights of two uncertain edges is correct. Its time complexity is* $O(k \log k)$.

Proof. The correctness of the algorithm follows from Theorem 5.2. The time complexity is $O(k \log k)$: computing the zonotopes $Z(s_i(q_a)), Z(s_j(q_a)), Z(s_l(q))$ takes $O(k \log k)$ time; computing the VDs (steps 2, 3) takes $O(k \log k)$ time; finding the farthest and closest vertices for each vertex of zonotope $Z(s_j(q_a))$ (steps 4, 5) takes $O(k \log k)$ time. The space complexity is $O(k)$.

□

Table 5.1.   Algorithm for comparing the weights of two uncertain edges.

Input: LPGUM edges $e_{jl}(q) = (s_j(q), s_l(q)), e_{ij}(q) = (s_i(q), s_j(q))$.

1. Compute the zonotopes $Z(s_i(q)), Z(s_j(q)), Z(s_l(q))$.
2. Compute the Farthest Point Voronoi diagram of the vertices $S_i = \langle p_{i1}, p_{i2}, \dots, p_{ik} \rangle$ of zonotope $Z(s_i(q))$.
3. Compute the Voronoi diagram of the vertices $S_l = \langle p_{l1}, p_{l2}, \dots, p_{lk} \rangle$ of zonotope $Z(s_l(q))$.
4. For each vertex of zonotope $Z(s_j(q))$, compute the minimum distance differences between the farthest from it in $S_i = \langle p_{i1}, p_{i2}, \dots, p_{ik} \rangle$ and the closest vertex from it in $S_l = \langle p_{l1}, p_{l2}, \dots, p_{lk} \rangle$.
5. **If** all the segments minimum distance differences are positive **then** return *TRUE*. **Else** return *FALSE*.

Output: *TRUE* if edge $e_{jl}(q)$ is heavier than $e_{ij}(q)$, *FALSE* otherwise.

5.3.2 Dependent case

When the LPGUM points are dependent, the edge weights are also dependent. Edge $e_{lm}(q)$ is heavier than edge $e_{ij}(q)$ iff its weight is larger than that of $e_{lm}(q)$ for every parameter instance $\min_{q \in \Delta}\{w(e_{lm}(q)) - w(e_{ij}(q))\} \geq 0$.

The sign of this expression is equivalent to the sign of

$$\min_{q \in \Delta}\{(w(e_{lm}(q)))^2 - (w(e_{ij}(q)))^2\}$$

$$= \min_{q \in \Delta}\{(w(e_{lm}(q)) - w(e_{ij}(q)))(w(e_{lm}(q)) + w(e_{ij}(q)))\}$$

Note that $s_i(q) = (\bar{s}_i + qA_i)$, $s_j(q) = (\bar{s}_j + qA_j)$, $s_l(q) = (\bar{s}_l + qA_l)$ $s_m(q) = (\bar{s}_m + qA_m)$, so we obtain

$$\min_{q \in \Delta}\{(w(e_{lm}(q)))^2 - (w(e_{ij}(q)))^2\}$$

$$= \min_{q \in \Delta}\{\|s_m(q) - s_l(q)\|^2 - \|s_j(q) - s_i(q)\|^2\}$$

Now, denote $A_1 = A_m - A_l$, $A_2 = A_j - A_i$, $b_1 = \bar{s}_l - \bar{s}_m$ and $b_2 = \bar{s}_i - \bar{s}_j$. Then,

$$\begin{cases} \min\limits_{q}\{\|qA_1 - b_1\|^2 - \|qA_2 - b_2\|^2\} \\ \text{s.t. } q_j^2 \leq (q_j^+)^2, \quad 1 \leq j \leq k \end{cases}$$

which is a Difference of Convex functions problem that is equivalent to

$$\begin{cases} \min\limits_{q \in \Delta}\{q(A_1 A_1^T - A_2 A_2^T)q^T - 2q(A_1 b_1 - A_2 b_2) + \|b_1\|^2 - \|b_2\|^2\} \\ \text{s.t. } q_j^2 \leq (q_j^+)^2, \quad 1 \leq j \leq k \end{cases}$$

Let $A = A_1 A_1^T - A_2 A_2^T$, $b = A_1 b_1 - A_2 b_2$, $c = \|b_1\|^2 - \|b_2\|^2$. Then,

$$\begin{cases} \min\limits_{q \in \Delta}\left\{ \begin{pmatrix} q^T \\ 1 \end{pmatrix} \begin{pmatrix} A & -b^T \\ -b & c \end{pmatrix} (q \ 1) \right\} \\ \text{s.t. } q_j^2 \leq (q_j^+)^2, \ 1 \leq j \leq k \end{cases}$$

Let $X = \begin{pmatrix} q^T \\ 1 \end{pmatrix}(q \ 1)$. Then, we obtain the following optimization problem:

$$\begin{cases} \min_{q \in \Delta} \left\{ Tr \left\{ X \begin{pmatrix} A & -b^T \\ -b & c \end{pmatrix} \right\} \right\} \\ \\ \text{s.t.} \begin{cases} q_j^2 \leq (q_j^+)^2, \ 1 \leq j \leq k \\ X \succeq 0 \end{cases} \end{cases}$$

Note that when $\begin{pmatrix} A & -b^T \\ -b & c \end{pmatrix} \succeq 0$, this problem is a semi-definite programming (SDP) problem that can be solved in polynomial time when $A \succeq 0$ and $b^T A^{-1} b - c \leq 0$ (Schur's Lemma). While quadratic optimization is NP-hard in the number of dimensions, Ye [72] showed that a 4/7-approximate solution can be obtained in polynomial time for a quadratic programming with bound and quadratic constraints. This approximate solution is applicable in our case. Thus, it remains an open problem to determine if this specific instance is also NP-hard. In the following, we denote by $T(k)$ the time complexity for solving this quadratic optimization problem.

5.4   Uncertain EMST Stability Test

We describe next three algorithms for testing the stability of an uncertain EMST. The first one is for both the independent and the dependent cases with time complexity of $O(n^3 k \log k)$ and $O(n^3 T(k))$, respectively, where $T(k)$ is the time complexity for solving a quadratic optimization problem. The next two are for the independent case and reduce the time complexity to $O(n^2 k \log k)$ and $O(nk \log nk \log n)$, respectively.

5.4.1   Stability test for independent and dependent cases

Definition 5.8. *Let $S(q) = \{s_1(q), \ldots, s_n(q)\}$ be a set of n LPGUM points and let $\mathrm{EMST}(S(q)) = (V(S(q)), T(q))$ be an uncertain EMST of it. We denote by $c_{ij}(q)$ the cycle created by adding an edge $e_{ij}(q) \notin T(q)e_{ij}(q) \in E(S(q))$ to $\mathrm{EMST}(S(q))$.*

Theorem 5.4. *The uncertain* $\mathrm{EMST}(S(q)) = (V(S(q)), T(q))$ *is said to be stable iff* $\forall e_{ij}(q) \notin T(q), e_{ij}(q) \in E(S(q))$ *the weight* $w(e_{ij}(q))$ *is greater than or equal to the weight* $w(e_{lm}(q))$, $\forall e_{lm}(q) \in c_{ij}(q)$.

Proof. $\implies$ Assume by contradiction that $\mathrm{EMST}(S(q))$ is stable, i.e., $\forall q_a \in \Delta$, $\mathrm{EMST}(S(q_a)) = \mathrm{EMST}(\bar{S})$, but there is an edge $e_{ij}(q) \notin T(q), e_{ij}(q) \in E(S(q))$ whose weight $w(e_{ij}(q))$ is smaller than the weight of $w(e_{lm}(q)), \forall e_{lm}(q) \in c_{ij}(q)$, i.e., $\exists q_b \in \Delta$ for which $w(e_{ij}(q_b)) < w(e_{lm}(q_b))$. Then, we can replace the edge $e_{lm}(q_b)$ by $e_{ij}(q_b)$ and obtain an EMST whose minimal weight is smaller. This is a contradiction to the weight minimality of $\mathrm{EMST}(S(q_b))$. Thus, $\mathrm{EMST}(S(q_b)) \neq \mathrm{EMST}(S(q_a))$, $\forall q_a \in \Delta$.

$\impliedby$ Assume that $\forall e_{ij}(q) \notin T(q), e_{ij}(q) \in E(S(q))$, the weight $w(e_{ij}(q))$ is greater than or equal to the weight $w(e_{lm}(q))$, $\forall e_{lm}(q) \in c_{ij}(q)$. Thus, $w(e_{ij}(q_a)) \geq w(e_{lm}(q_a))$, $\forall q_a$ and $\forall e_{lm}(q) \in c_{ij}(q)$, therefore $e_{ij}(q_a) \notin T(q_a)$ and $\mathrm{EMST}(S(q_a)) = \mathrm{EMST}(\bar{S})$, $\forall q_a \in \Delta$. □

Assume first that $\mathrm{EMST}(\bar{S})$ is unique. Table 5.2 lists an algorithm for both the independent and the dependent cases with time complexity of $O(n^3 k \log k)$ and $O(n^3 T(k))$, respectively, that follows directly from Theorem 5.4.

Table 5.2. Algorithm for testing the stability of an uncertain EMST.

Input: A set of n LPGUM points $S(q) = \{s_1(q), s_2(q), \ldots, s_n(q)\}$ and its nominal Euclidian minimum spanning tree $\mathrm{EMST}(\bar{S}) = (\bar{V}, \bar{T})$

1. Compute the zonotopes $Z(s_1(q)), \ldots, Z(s_n(q))$.
2. Initialize $\mathrm{EMST}(S(q)) = (V(S(q)), T(q))$ to $\mathrm{EMST}(\bar{S}) = (\bar{V}, \bar{S})$.
3. For each edge $e_{ij}(q) \in E(q)$ in the Euclidean graph $G(S(q)) = (V(S(q), E(q))$ that is not in the tree, $e_{ij}(q) \notin T(q)$ add it to $\mathrm{EMST}(S(q))$, thereby creating a cycle $c_{ij}(q)$.
4. For each edge $e_{lm}(q)$ on the cycle $c_{ij}(q)$, compare the weights of $w(e_{lm}(q))$ and $w(e_{ij}(q))$.
5. **If** there exists an edge $e_{lm}(q) \in c_{ij}(q)$ such that $\exists q_a \in \Delta$ for which $w(e_{lm}(q_a)) > w(e_{ij}(q_a))$, **then** return *UNSTABLE*. **Else**, return *STABLE*.

Output: *STABLE* if $\mathrm{EMST}(S(q)) = (V(S(q)), T(q))$ is stable, otherwise *UNSTABLE*.

Next, we consider the case where there is more than one $\mathrm{EMST}(\bar{S})$. We distinguish between the independent and the dependent cases.

5.4.1.1   *Independent case*

Theorem 5.5. *Let* $\overline{\mathrm{EMST}} = \mathrm{EMST}(\bar{S}) = (\bar{V}, \bar{T}), \overline{\mathrm{EMST}'} = \mathrm{EMST}'(\bar{S}) = (\bar{V}, \bar{T}')$ *be two different nominal EMST defined on the same LPGUM point set* $S(q)$. *When the nominal* $\overline{\mathrm{EMST}}$ *is not unique, then either both uncertain* $\mathrm{EMST}(S(q))$ *are stable or both are unstable unless* $\exists \bar{e}_{ij} \in \bar{T}, \bar{e}_{ij} \notin \bar{T}'$ *such that*

$$\mathrm{min\_dist}(s_i(q), s_j(q)) = \mathrm{dist}(\bar{s}_i, \bar{s}_j) \neq \mathrm{max\_dist}(s_i(q), s_j(q))$$

Proof.   When all the endpoints of all the edges such that $\bar{e}_{ij} \in \bar{T}, \bar{e}_{ij} \notin \bar{T}'$ and $\bar{e}_{ml} \in \bar{T}', \bar{e}_{ml} \notin \bar{T}$ are independent of all parameters, i.e.,

$$A_i = \begin{pmatrix} 0 & 0 \\ \vdots & \vdots \\ 0 & 0 \end{pmatrix}, A_j = \begin{pmatrix} 0 & 0 \\ \vdots & \vdots \\ 0 & 0 \end{pmatrix}, A_l = \begin{pmatrix} 0 & 0 \\ \vdots & \vdots \\ 0 & 0 \end{pmatrix}, A_m = \begin{pmatrix} 0 & 0 \\ \vdots & \vdots \\ 0 & 0 \end{pmatrix}$$

then all the common edges in both trees $\mathrm{EMST}(S(q))$ and $\mathrm{EMST}'(S(q))$, $\bar{e}_{ij} \in \bar{T}, \bar{e}_{ij} \notin \bar{T}'$ are identical. Thus, either both trees $\mathrm{EMST}(S(q)), \mathrm{EMST}'(S(q))$ are stable or both trees are unstable.

Otherwise, $\exists \bar{e}_{ij} \in \bar{T}, \bar{e}_{ij} \notin \bar{T}'$ such that $s_i(q)$ or $s_j(q)$ or both depend on at least one parameter. We add $\bar{e}_{ij}$ to $\overline{EMST'}$, thereby creating a cycle $\bar{c}'_{ij}$. So, (1) the weight of $\bar{e}_{ij}$ is heavier than that all the edges in the cycle $\bar{c}'_{ij}$ and (2) there is at least another edge $\bar{e}'_{lm} \in \bar{c}'_{ij}$ with equal weight.

Deleting the edge $\bar{e}_{ij}$ from $\overline{\mathrm{EMST}}$ creates a graph with two connected components, cc_i, cc_j. The components cc_i, cc_j are disjoint and define a cut of $\overline{\mathrm{EMST}}$. The weight of the edge $\bar{e}_{ij}$ is minimal of all edges in the Euclidean graph $\bar{G}$ that connects the two components cc_i, cc_j. Since $\bar{c}'_{ij}$ is a cycle, $\exists \bar{e}'_{lm} \in \bar{c}'_{ij}$ other than $\bar{e}_{ij}$ which also connects between the two components cc_i, cc_j.

Since we assume that uncertainty intervals are zero-centered symmetric, the edge weights can be increased and decreased independently. The idea is first to find $q_a \in \Delta$ for which $e_{ij}(q_a)$ is lighter than that of $\bar{e}_{ij}$ and thus for $q_a \in \Delta$, $e_{ij}(q_a)$ is necessarily an edge in an EMST. Second, we find $q_b \in \Delta$ for which $e_{ij}(q_b)$ is heavier

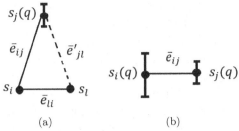

(a)　　　　　　　　　(b)

Fig. 5.6. Illustration of the cases in Theorem 5.5: (a) exact points s_i, s_l, LPGUM point $s_j(q)$ and its uncertainty zone (vertical interval, solid line), nominal edges $\bar{e}_{ij}, \bar{e}_{li}$ of $\overline{\text{EMST}}$ (solid lines) and nominal edge $\bar{e}'_{jl}$ of $\overline{\text{EMST}}'$ (dashed line) such that $w(\bar{e}_{ij}) = w(\bar{e}'_{jl})$ and $\forall q_a \in \Delta, w(e_{ij}(q_a)) = w(e'_{jl}(q_a))$; (b) LPGUM points $s_j(q), s_i(q)$, their uncertainty zones (vertical solid line interval) and nominal edge $\bar{e}_{ij}$ (solid line) such that min_dist$(s_i(q), s_j(q)) = $dist$(\bar{s}_i, \bar{s}_j) \neq$ max_dist$(s_i(q), s_j(q))$.

than $\bar{e}_{ij}$ and thus for $q_b \in \Delta$, $e_{ij}(q_b)$ is necessarily not an edge in an EMST. Thus, $\exists e_{ij}(q) \in E(S(q))$ such that for a parameter vector instance $q_a \in \Delta, e_{ij}(q_a) \in T(q_a)$ and $q_b \in \Delta, e_{ij}(q_b) \notin T(q_b)$. Therefore, EMST$(S(q))$ is unstable.

This property holds for all LPGUM points except for two special cases shown in Fig. 5.6. We discuss them next.

Case 1: The neighbor edge of $\bar{e}_{ij}$, denoted by $\bar{e}'_{jl}$, shares endpoint $s_j(q)$ with $\bar{e}_{ij}$. Thus, edges $e_{ij}(q)$ and $e'_{jl}(q)$ are dependent — the dependency is such that for every parameter instance their weights are equal, i.e., $\exists \bar{e}'_{jl} \in \bar{c}'_{ij}$ such that $w(\bar{e}_{ij}) = w(\bar{e}'_{jl})$ and $\forall q_a \in \Delta, w(e_{ij}(q_a)) = w(e'_{jl}(q_a))$. In this case, $q_a \in \Delta$ for which $e_{ij}(q_a)$ is the only edge with the largest weight in the cycle $c'_{ij}(q)$, $\nexists q_a \in \Delta$ for which $w(e_{ij}(q_a)) < w(e'_{jl}(q_a))$. Therefore, if the remaining edges in EMST$(S(q))$ and in EMST$'(S(q))$ are stable, then both trees such that $e_{ij}(q) \in T(q)$ and $e_{ij}(q) \notin T'(q)$ are stable.

Case 2: The weight of the edge $\bar{e}_{ij}$ cannot be decreased for every parameter vector instance, i.e., min_dist$(s_i(q), s_j(q)) = $dist$(\bar{s}_i, \bar{s}_j) \neq$ max_dist$(s_i(q), s_j(q))$. In this case, $\exists q_a$ such that $w(e_{ij}(q_a)) > w(\bar{e}_{ij})$. Therefore, $\exists q_a \in \Delta$ for which $e_{ij}(q_a) \in T(q_a)$ and the EMST$(S(q))$ for which $e_{ij}(q) \in T(q)$ is unstable, but if the remaining edges in EMST$'(S(q))$ are stable, then the EMST$'(S(q))$ for which $e_{ij}(q) \notin T'(q)$ is stable. $\qquad \square$

Therefore, if the EMST is not unique, we can test that for all the edges $e_{ij}(q) \in T(q)$ in $\text{EMST}(S(q))$ that $\text{min\_dist}(s_i(q), s_j(q)) = \text{dist}(\bar{s}_i, \bar{s}_j) \neq \text{max\_dist}(s_i(q), s_j(q))$. Without loss of generality, when $s_i(q)$ depends only on one parameter, $s_j(q)$ depends on at most one parameter and $\bar{e}_{ij}$ is perpendicular to $Z(s_i(q))$ and $Z(s_j(q))$. This can be tested in $O(nk)$ time. If there is no such edge, we can arbitrarily choose one EMST and apply the algorithm listed in Table 5.2. This additional test does not change the overall time complexity of $O(n^3 k \log k)$ of the algorithm.

5.4.1.2 *Dependent case*

In contrast to the independent case, when we reduce or increase the weight of edge $\bar{e}_{ij} \in \bar{E}$ in a dependent nominal Euclidean graph, all the other edges $\bar{e}_{ml} \in \bar{E}$ may change their weight too due to their mutual parameter dependencies. Therefore, if there is more than a single EMST, some of them may be stable, while others may be unstable. We can test the stability of each EMST with the algorithm listed in Table 5.2.

Theorem 5.6. *Let $S(q)$ be a point set. Let $\bar{T}_1, \ldots, \bar{T}_m$ be m nominal EMSTs defined on $\bar{S}$ such that the corresponding LPGUM trees $T_1(q), \ldots, T_m(q)$ are all stable. Then, for all $1 \leq, i, j \leq m$ and all choices of $q_a \in \Delta$, the weights of $w(T_i(q_a))$ and $w(T_j(q_a))$ are the same.*

Proof. By contradiction, suppose that $\exists q_a \in \Delta$ such that $w(T_i(q_a)) < w(T_j(q_a))$. Consider the point set instance $S(q_a)$. By definition, $T_j(q_a)$ is not an EMST because there exists an EMST $T_i(q_a)$ whose weight is smaller. Thus, $T_j(q_a) \neq \bar{T}_j$, a contradiction to the stability of $T_j(q)$. □

5.4.2 Stability test with lower complexity
for the independent case

Table 5.3 lists an algorithm that improves the complexity of the stability test by reducing the number of edge weight comparison tests. We compare every edge of the Euclidean graph $G(S(q)) = (V(S(q)), E(S(q)))$ that is not in the EMST, $e_{ij}(q) \in E(S(q)), e_{ij}(q) \notin T(q)$ with three edges: two neighbor edges on the cycle $c_{ij}(q)$ and the heaviest edge in $c_{ij}(q)$ of $\text{EMST}(S(q))$. If $e_{ij}(q)$

Table 5.3.   Algorithm for testing the stability of an independent EMST.

Input: A set of n LPGUM points $S(q) = \{s_1(q), s_2(q), \ldots, s_n(q)\}$, and a nominal Euclidian minimum spanning tree $\text{EMST}(\bar{S}) = (\bar{V}, \bar{T})$

1. Compute the zonotopes $Z(s_1(q)), Z(s_2(q)), \ldots, Z(s_n(q))$.
2. Initialize $\text{EMST}(S(q)) = (V(S(q)), T(q))$ to $\text{EMST}(\bar{S}) = (\bar{V}, \bar{S})$.
3. For each edge $e_{lm}(q) \in T(q)$ compute max $\_\text{dist}(s_l(q), s_m(q))$.
4. For each edge on the uncertain Euclidean graph $G(S(q)) = (V(S(q)), E(q))$ that is not in the EMST $e_{ij}(q) \in E(q)$, $e_{ij}(q) \notin T(q)$ add it to $\text{EMST}(S(q))$, thereby creating a cycle $c_{ij}(q)$.
5. Compare the weight $w(e_{ij}(q))$ with its two neighbors edges on the cycle $c_{ij}(q)$ and with another edge of $\text{EMST}(S(q))$ with the heaviest max $\_\text{dist}(s_l(q), s_m(q))$ in $c_{ij}(q)$.
6. **If** $e_{ij}(q)$ is heavier than the three edges in step 5, **then** return *STABLE*. **Else**, return *UNSTABLE*.

Output: *STABLE* if $\text{EMST}(S(q)) = (V(S(q)), T(q))$ is stable, otherwise *UNSTABLE*.

---

is heavier than all tree edges, then it does not decrease the EMST total weight.

Denote by $e_{ij}(q) \in E(S(q)), e_{ij}(q) \notin T(q)$ the current edge added to the EMST and by $e_{lm}(q)$ the edge in $c_{ij}(q)$ of $\text{EMST}(S(q))$ with the heaviest weight. The point uncertainties are independent and $e_{ij}(q)$ is disjoint to any other edge in $c_{ij}(q)$. If $\exists e_{rt}(q) \in c_{ij}(q)$ and $\exists q_a \in \Delta$ such that $w(e_{ij}(q_a)) < w(e_{rt}(q_a))$, then:

$$\min\_\text{dist}(s_i(q), s_j(q)) \leq w(e_{ij}(q_a)) < w(e_{rt}(q_a))$$
$$\leq \max\_\text{dist}(s_l(q), s_m(q))$$

Thus, $\min\_\text{dist}(s_i(q), s_j(q)) < \max\_\text{dist}(s_l(q), s_m(q))$ and edge $e_{ij}(q)$ is not heavier than edge $e_{lm}(q)$, Thus, the EMST is unstable.

Hagerup [73] describes a linear time algorithm for the tree-path-maxima problem of a tree with real edge weights and a list of pairs of distinct nodes. Computing for each pair of nodes a maximum weight edge on the path in the tree between the nodes takes $O(n)$ time. Thus, by a preprocessing of $O(n)$ time on the heaviest weight for each edge $e_{ij}(q) \in T(q)$, the heaviest edge in $c_{ij}(q)$ is found in constant time.

Theorem 5.7. *The algorithm listed in Table 5.3 for testing the stability of independent* $\text{EMST}(S(q))$ *is correct. Its time complexity is* $O(n^2 k \log k)$.

Proof. In step 4 of the algorithm, we compare the weight of the new added edge, $w(e_{ij}(q))$, to that of its two neighboring edges because they share a common point and thus their weight depends on the weight of $w(e_{ij}(q))$. We omit the rest of the proof of correctness in the interest of space, as it is straightforward.

The time complexity proof is as follows. Computing the zono-topes $Z(s_1(q)), \ldots, Z(s_n(q))$ requires $O(nk \log k)$ time. Computing the $\max\_\mathrm{dist}(s_l(q), s_m(q))$ for an edge $e_{lm}(q) \in T(q)$ requires $O(k)$ time. Since there are $n - 1$ edges in EMST$(S(q))$, the time required to compute the maximum distances is $O(nk)$. Since there are $O(n^2)$ edges in the uncertain Euclidean graph $G(S(q))$ that are not in the Euclidean minimum spanning tree EMST$(S(q))$, i.e., $e_{ij}(q) \in E(S(q)), e_{ij}(q) \notin T(q)$. We compare every such edge with tree edges in cost of $O(k \log k)$ time. Overall, the comparisons take $O(n^2 k \log k)$ time and $O(n^2 + nk)$ space. $\square$

5.4.3   Recursive stability test for the independent case

We now describe a recursive algorithm for testing the stability of independent uncertain EMST with an improved time complexity of $O(nk \log nk \log n)$. Table 5.4 lists the algorithm. It improves the time complexity by reducing the number of edges $e_{ij}(q) \notin T(q)$ to be tested. The algorithm is described and proved in two stages: first for the case where the independent EMST$(S(q))$ is a full balanced binary tree, and then for the general case by showing how to convert an unbalanced EMST tree into a full balanced tree with no time and space complexity penalty.

Theorem 5.8. *The algorithm listed in Table 5.4 for testing the stability of independent full balanced binary* EMST$(S(q))$ *is correct. Its time complexity is* $O(nk \log nk \log n)$.

Proof. By induction on the depth of EMST$(S(q))$, the basis of the induction is a tree of depth 1. In this case, there is only one edge $e_{ij}(q) \notin T(q)$ that may cause the instability of the tree. This edge connects between the nodes $s_i(q) \in T_L$ and $s_j(q) \in T_R$. In step 4 of the procedure ***IS_STABLE***(T), edge $e_{ij}(q)$ is chosen as the one with the minimum weight since it is the only edge that does not

Table 5.4. Algorithm for testing the stability of an independent uncertain EMST.

$STABILITY_TEST$$(S(q), \text{EMST}(\bar{S}))$

Input: A set of n LPGUM points $S(q) = \{s_1(q), s_2(q), \ldots, s_n(q)\}$ and a nominal Euclidian minimum spanning tree $\text{EMST}(\bar{S}) = (\bar{V}, \bar{S})$

1. Compute the zonotopes $Z(s_1(q)), Z(s_2(q)), \ldots, Z(s_n(q))$.
2. Initialize $\text{EMST}(S(q)) = (V(S(q)), T(q))$ to $\text{EMST}(\bar{S}) = (\bar{V}, \bar{S})$.
3. For each edge $e_{lm}(q) \in T(q)$ compute max $\_dist(s_l(q), s_m(q))$.
4. Process $\text{EMST}(S(q))$ to answer tree-path-maxima problem queries.
5. Compute the Voronoi diagram of the zonotopes
   $Z(s_1(q)), Z(s_2(q)), \ldots, Z(s_n(q))$.
6. Return **IS_STABLE**$(\text{EMST}(S(q)))$.

Output: *STABLE* if $\text{EMST}(S(q)) = (V(S(q)), T(q))$ is stable, otherwise *UNSTABLE*.

$IS_STABLE$$(T)$
Input: An Euclidian minimum spanning tree $T = \text{EMST}(S(q))$

1. Split T into left and right sub-trees T_L and T_R.
2. Add the root node point $s_r(q)$ of T to both sub-trees as their root.
3. **If** T_L and T_R are not leaves, **then**
   ($IS\_STABLE(T_L)$ and $IS\_STABLE(T_R)$).
4. For each node $s_i(q) \in T_L$ find a node $s_j(q) \in T_R$ such that $e_{ij}(q) \notin T$ and the min $\_dist(s_i(q), s_j(q))$ is the minimal out of all $s_j(q) \in T_R$.
5. Compare the weight $w(e_{ij}(q))$ with its two neighbors edges on the cycle $c_{ij}(q)$ and with another edge $e_{lm}(q)$ on the path from $s_i(q)$ to $s_j(q)$ with the heaviest max $\_dist(s_l(q), s_m(q))$.
6. Repeat steps 4 and 5 for each node $s_i(q) \in T_R$.
7. **If** for each node $s_i(q) \in T_L$ and $s_i(q) \in T_R$, $w(e_{lm}(q))$ is heavier than $w(e_{ij}(q))$, **then** return *STABLE*. **Else**, return *UNSTABLE*.

Output: *STABLE* if $\text{EMST}(S(q)) = (V(S(q)), T(q))$ is stable, otherwise *UNSTABLE*.

---

belong to the tree. Then, in step 5, this edge is compared to the two neighboring edges. As in the basis case, the tree contains only these two neighboring edges, and the procedure will detect the stability or instability of the tree. By induction, we assume that the procedure will detect the stability or instability of $\text{EMST}(S(q))$ of depth $h - 1$. We now prove that it is also true for $\text{EMST}(S(q))$ whose depth is h.

Let $\text{EMST}(S(q))$ be a tree whose depth is h. Let $s_r(q)$ be the root node of the $\text{EMST}(S(q))$. We split $\text{EMST}(S(q))$ into its left and right sub-trees, T_L and T_R. By the induction assumption, we independently test the stability of T_L and T_R. It then remains to test the edges $e_{ij}(q) \notin T(q), s_i(q) \in T_L, s_j(q) \in T_R$. The edge $e_{ij}(q) \notin T$ is a witness to the instability of T iff $\exists e_{ab}(q) \in c_{ij}(q)$ such that $w(e_{ab}(q))$ is not lighter than $w(e_{ij}(q))$, i.e., $\min\_dist(s_i(q), s_j(q)) < \max\_dist(s_a(q), s_b(q))$.

Figure 5.7 illustrates the following situations. Let $e_{lm}(q)$ be the heaviest edge in the path from $s_i(q)$ to $s_r(q)$ in T_L and let $e_{uv}(q)$ be the heaviest edge in the path from $s_j(q)$ to $s_r(q)$ in T_R. By definition,

$$\max\_dist(s_a(q), s_b(q)) \leq \max\_dist(s_l(q), s_m(q))$$

$$\text{or } \max\_dist(s_a(q), s_b(q)) \leq \max\_dist(s_u(q), s_v(q)).$$

Suppose that $\max\_dist(s_a(q), s_b(q)) \leq \max\_dist(s_l(q), s_m(q))$ and let $e_{id}(q) \notin T$ be the edge with the minimal distance from $s_i(q)$ to the closest node in T_R. Thus,

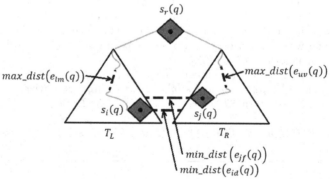

Fig. 5.7.   Illustration of the proof of Theorem 5.8. Point $s_r(q)$ is the root node of the $\text{EMST}(S(q))$. T_R and T_L are left and right sub-trees. Points $s_i(q) \in T_L$ and $s_j(q) \in T_R$. In black dotted lines are (1) the maximum distance of the heaviest edge in the path from $s_i(q)$ to $s_r(q)$ in T_L; (2) the maximum distance of the heaviest edge in the path from $s_j(q)$ to $s_r(q)$ in T_R; (3) the minimal distance from $s_i(q)$ to the closest node $s_d(q) \in T_R$; (4) the minimal distance from $s_j(q)$ to the closest node $s_f(q) \in T_L$. In gray lines are the paths in $\text{EMST}(S(q))$.

$$\text{min \_dist}(s_i(q), s_d(q)) \leq \text{min \_dist}(s_i(q), s_j(q))$$

$$\text{and min \_dist}(s_i(q), s_d(q)) \leq \text{max \_dist}(s_l(q), s_m(q)).$$

Suppose now that $\text{max \_dist}(s_a(q), s_b(q)) \leq \text{max \_dist}(s_u(q), s_v(q))$ and let $e_{jf}(q) \notin T$ be the edge with the minimal distance from $s_j(q)$ to the closest node in T_L. Thus,

$$\text{min \_dist}(s_j(q), s_f(q)) \leq \text{min \_dist}(s_i(q), s_j(q))$$

$$\text{and min \_dist}(s_j(q), s_f(q)) \leq \text{max \_dist}(s_u(q), s_v(q)).$$

Therefore, it suffices to test only the edge with the minimal distance from $s_i(q)$ to the closest node in T_R and the edge with the minimal distance from $s_j(q)$ to the closest node in T_L. That is, it suffices to test only one edge for each node in T_R and T_L.

Complexity. Computing the zonotopes $Z(s_1(q)), \ldots, Z(s_n(q))$ takes $O(nk \log k)$ time. For each edge $e_{lm}(q) \in T(q)$, computing its maximum weight takes $O(k)$ time, overall $O(nk)$. Processing EMST$(S(q))$ to answer tree-path-maxima queries takes $O(n)$ time with the method described in [73]. Computing the VD of the zonotopes $Z(s_1(q)), \ldots, Z(s_n(q))$ takes $O(n \log nk)$, where n is the number of the polygons and nk is sum of the vertices of the zonotopes [5]. Overall, $O(nk \log k + n \log nk) = O(nk \log k + n \log n)$ time and $O(nk)$ space are required for $\textbf{STABILITY\_TEST}(S(q), \text{EMST}(\bar{S}))$.

The complexity of the recursive procedure $\textbf{IS\_STABLE}$ (EMST$(S(q))$) is as follows. For each node $s_i(q) \in T_L$, we find a node $s_j(q) \in T_R$ such that $e_{ij}(q) \notin T$ and $\text{min \_dist}(s_i(q), s_j(q))$ is the minimal of all $s_j(q) \in T_R$; for each node $s_j(q) \in T_R$, we find a node $s_i(q) \in T_L$ such that $e_{ij}(q) \notin T$ and the $\text{min \_dist}(s_i(q), s_j(q))$ is the minimal of all $s_i(q) \in T_L$. These computations require $O(nk \log n)$ time with the zonotope VD method described in [5]. Since there are $O(\log n)$ nodes that are neighbors of the other sub-tree, the complexity of each node is $O(k)$. Notice that for every node $s_a(q)$, the closest nodes in the corresponding sub-tree are the ones that are neighbors of $s_a(q)$ in the zonotope VD. Since the tree is a full binary tree, there are $O(\log n)$ such nodes in the corresponding sub-tree of $s_a(q)$. The closest edge is incident to one of these nodes, so it also takes $O(k \log n)$ time to find it.

Finding the heaviest edge in the path from $s_i(q)$ to $s_j(q)$ takes constant time based on the preprocessing. Thus, finding the heaviest edge for every node in the tree takes $O(n)$ time. Comparing three edges for each node takes $O(nk \log k)$ time. Overall, $T(n) = 2T(\frac{n}{2}) + O(nk \log nk) = O(nk \log nk \log n)$. Therefore, the total time complexity is $O(nk \log k + n \log nk + nk \log nk \log n) = O(nk \log k + n \log n + n \log k + nk \log nk \log n) = O(nk \log nk \log n)$. $\qquad\square$

Next, we extend this result to the general case in which $\text{EMST}(S(q))$ may be unbalanced.

Theorem 5.9. *The algorithm listed in Table 5.4 for testing the stability of independent $\text{EMST}(S(q))$ with an additional preprocessing step and modified steps 1 and 4 of the procedure **IS_STABLE**(T) is correct. Its time complexity is $O(nk \log nk \log n)$.*

Proof. The preprocessing stage converts the nominal EMST into a binary EMST by recursively adding $O(n)$ auxiliary nodes as follows (Fig. 5.8). The nodes of the nominal EMST are recursively visited from the root to the leaves. When the current node $s_i(q)$ has two children, no changes are made. When it has a single child, a new node is added as its second child. When it has more than two children, $l > 2$, then node $s_i(q)$ is redefined so its leftmost child is its left child node and the right node is a new added node, $s_{\text{new}}(q)$. The remaining children of $s_i(q)$ are redefined to be the children of $s_{\text{new}}(q)$. This procedure continues until only two children remain. This adds $l - 2$ auxiliary nodes for each node with more than two children. The result is a binary tree with $O(n)$ auxiliary nodes.

The algorithm of Table 5.4 applies to the general case of unbalanced EMSTs, as it does not rely on the tree being balanced. However, its complexity is higher, as the tree depth can be $O(n)$. To avoid this, we show next how to convert the unbalanced binary tree into a full balanced binary tree, one whose depth is $O(\log n)$.

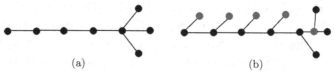

(a)   (b)

Fig. 5.8. Illustration of the conversion of an EMST into a binary tree: (a) an EMST; (b) the converted tree. In black are the original nodes and in gray are the auxiliary nodes.

In the first step of each stage of the recursion, we find the middle node $s_m(q) \in V(S(q))$ such that at least $\frac{n}{c}, c \in N, c \geq 2$, and no more than $\frac{(c-1)n}{c}$ nodes are its children, where n is the number of nodes in the tree $|V(S(q))| = n$. We make $s_p(q)$, the parent of $s_m(q)$ in $V(S(q))$, into a new root of $T = EMST(S(q))$. Now T_L and T_R are of comparable size up to a constant factor of c.

We use both the original EMST and the converted full binary tree. In the procedure $\boldsymbol{STABILITY\_TEST}(S(q), \text{EMST}(\bar{S}))$, all the steps are performed on the original unbalanced EMST. The call to $\boldsymbol{IS\_STABLE}(T)$ is performed on the converted full binary tree. Then, the middle node $s_m(q)$ is identified and the tree is split into left and right sub-trees. Note that since all the nodes of the original unbalanced EMST are present in the converted full binary tree, the partition properly defines which nodes belong to left and right sub-trees. Step 2 in $\boldsymbol{IS\_STABLE}(T)$ is performed on the middle node parent, $s_p(q)$. All the remaining steps are performed on the original unbalanced EMST.

Since the EMST is not necessarily a balanced one, we cannot assume that there are $O(\log n)$ nodes that are neighbors of the other sub-tree. Therefore, step 4 of the procedure $\boldsymbol{IS\_STABLE}(T)$ is modified as follows.

Consider the VD that was computed in step 5 of the procedure $\boldsymbol{STABILITY\_TEST}(S(q), \text{EMST}(\bar{S}))$. We distinguish between the zonotopes (nodes) of T_L that are neighbors of zonotopes (nodes) of T_R, i.e., zonotopes that share a common edge with the zonotopes on the other sub-tree, and nodes of T_L that are not neighbors of nodes of T_R.

First, we find the node with minimum distance for the nodes that share a common edge with the other sub-tree in the zonotope VD. Notice that for every node $s_a(q)$, the closest nodes in the corresponding sub-tree are the ones that are neighbors of $s_a(q)$ in the zonotope VD. The closest edge is incident to one of these nodes, so it takes $O(k)$ time on average to find it. Since the average number of neighbors is constant and in the worst case at most $n - 1$ for a constant number of cases, the overall complexity is $O(nk)$.

Next, we apply Dijkstra's algorithm for the nodes that do not share a common edge with the other sub-tree. We describe the steps for the nodes of T_R; the steps for the nodes in T_L are identical.

(1) Mark all the nodes of T_R that share a common edge with the nodes of T_L as visited, add a pointer to the closest node in T_L and update their minimum distance to T_L accordingly. Mark all the remaining nodes of T_R as unvisited and update their distance to T_L as ∞.

(2) Consider the Delaunay triangulation defined by the VD. For each visited node $s_a(q)$ that shares a common edge in the Delaunay triangulation with unvisited node $s_b(q)$ in T_R, compute the minimum distance between $s_b(q)$ and the closest node of $s_a(q)$ in T_L. Then, compare the current distance of $s_b(q)$ from T_L and the previous one and update the current node to the closest distance and update its pointer to that of the corresponding node in T_L.

(3) After updating all the unvisited neighbor nodes in the Delaunay triangulation, choose the unvisited node with the smallest distance to T_L, label it as visited and continue to step two until all the nodes in T_R are marked as visited.

Note that the Delaunay triangulation defined by the VD has $O(n)$ edges and vertices, so Dijkstra's algorithm requires $O(n \log n)$ steps. In each step, the closest distance between two zonotopes is computed in $O(k)$ time. Therefore, the overall time complexity remains $O(nk \log n)$.

Note also that the preprocessing and the modifications to the procedure **IS_STABLE**(T) do not affect the correctness of the algorithm in Table 5.4, so Theorem 5.9 follows from the correctness proof of the full balanced binary tree in Theorem 5.8.

Complexity. There is no time complexity penalty for converting the EMST tree to a binary one. The complexity of **STABILITY_TEST**$(S(q), \mathrm{EMST}(\bar{S}))$ is the same as in Theorem 5.8. The complexity of the modified steps 1 and 4 remains the same as in Theorem 5.8, and the total time complexity is $O(nk \log nk \log n)$. $\square$

5.5   The Weight of an Uncertain EMST

We describe next a method for computing the minimum and maximum weight of a stable uncertain EMST for the independent and dependent cases. The weight of a stable uncertain EMST is by definition the sum of its edge weights. Since the edges share common points, the edge weights are always dependent. This yields a quadratic optimization problem. The minimum weight of a stable EMST$(S(q))$ is defined as

$$\min_{q \in \Delta} \left\{ \sum_{e_{ij}(q) \in T(q)} w(e_{ij}(q)) \right\} = \min_{q \in \Delta} \left\{ \sum_{e_{ij}(q) \in T(q)} \|s_j(q) - s_i(q)\| \right\}$$

Note that $s_i(q) = (\bar{s}_i + qA_i)$, $s_j(q) = (\bar{s}_j + qA_j)$. Now, let $\bar{s} = \bar{s}_j - \bar{s}_i$ and $A = A_j - A_i$. Thus,

$$\begin{cases} \min_{q \in \Delta} \left\{ \sum_{e_{ij}(q) \in T(q)} \|qA + \bar{s}\| \right\} \\ \text{s.t.} \quad q_j^- \leq q_j \leq q_j^+, 1 \leq j \leq k \end{cases}$$

which is a k-dimensional bounded quadratic optimization problem with box constraints. In its general form, quadratic optimization is NP-hard. But, this problem is a Second-Order Cone Programming (SOCP) [74] and can be solved in $O(N^3)$ time, where $N = \max\{k, n\}$.

5.6 Summary

We have defined the uncertain EMST stability of n LPGUM points modeled with k real valued uncertainty parameters. We proved that when the uncertain EMST is unstable, it may have an exponential number of topologically different instances, thus precluding its polynomial time computation. We have presented algorithms for comparing two edge weights defined by the distance between the edge endpoints for the independent and dependent cases with time complexity of $O(k \log k)$ and $O(T(k))$, respectively, where $T(k)$ is the time required to solve a quadratic optimization problem with k parameters. We described an uncertain EMST stability test algorithm whose time complexity is $O(n^3 k \log k)$ and $O(nk + T(k))$ for the independent and dependent cases, respectively. We then presented a more efficient $O(nk \log nk \log n)$ time algorithm for the independent case and a method for computing the minimum and maximum total weight whose complexity is $O(N^3)$ time, where $N = \max\{k, n\}$.

Chapter 6

Voronoi Diagram and Delaunay Triangulation

This chapter addresses the problems of constructing the Voronoi diagram (VD) and Delaunay triangulation (DT) of points in the plane with mutually dependent location uncertainties. Section 6.1 presents the background. Section 6.2 defines an uncertain VD and uncertain DT. Section 6.3 defines the LPGUM bisector. Section 6.4 describes the intersection of two LPGUM lines. Section 6.5 defines the uncertain VD vertex. Section 6.6 describes an efficient algorithm for computing a stable uncertain VD. Section 6.7 describes the exact and uncertain LPGUM point location queries. Section 6.8 describes how to efficiently update a stable uncertain VD by inserting or deleting an LPGUM point. Section 6.9 summarizes the results.

6.1 Background

A variety of models and representations have been proposed to model the VD and the Delaunay triangulation (DT) of points in the plane in the presence of geometric uncertainty. Section 1.2 presents a review of the relevant literature.

Next, we motivate the problem and emphasize the importance of geometric uncertainty dependencies with the following example.

Figure 6.1 illustrates in-circle point classification with independent and dependent geometric uncertainty. Let the parametric uncertainty model $(q, \overline{q}\Delta)$ be defined by three parameters $(k = 3)$ and a vector $q = (q_1, q_2, q_3)$, where $\Delta_1 = \Delta_2 = \Delta_3 = [-1, 1]$. Let s_4 be

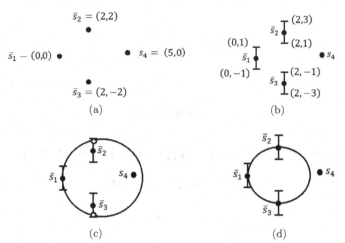

Fig. 6.1.   Example that illustrates that ignoring the point location uncertainty dependencies leads to an incorrect classification: (a) point $s_4 = (5,0)$ is an exact point and points $s_1(q), s_2(q), s_3(q)$ are three uncertain points whose nominal locations are $\bar{s}_1 = (0,0), \bar{s}_2 = (2,2), \bar{s}_3 = (2,-2)$ (black dots); (b) the location uncertainty of points $s_1(q), s_2(q), s_3(q)$ are vertical line intervals whose vertices are $(0,1)$ and $(0,-1)$, $(2,3)$ and $(2,1)$, $(2,-1)$ and $(2,-3)$ (black lines); (c) independent case: s_4 is inside the three-point circle defined by parameter vector instance $q_a = (0,1,-1)$, i.e., $s_1(q_a) = (0,0)$ (black dot), $s_2(q_a) = (2,3)$ and $s_3(q_a) = (2,-3)$ (white dots); (d) dependent case: s_4 is outside the three-point circle defined by the nominal point instances $\bar{s}_1, \bar{s}_2, \bar{s}_3$.

an exact point and let $s_1(q), s_2(q), s_3(q)$ be three uncertain points whose nominal locations are $\bar{s}_1, \bar{s}_2, \bar{s}_3$ (Fig. 6.1(a)). Let the sensitivity matrices of points $s_1(q), s_2(q), s_3(q)$ be $A_1^T = \begin{pmatrix} 0 & 0 & 0 \\ 1 & 0 & 0 \end{pmatrix}, A_1^T = \begin{pmatrix} 0 & 0 & 0 \\ 0 & 1 & 0 \end{pmatrix}, A_1^T = \begin{pmatrix} 0 & 0 & 0 \\ 0 & 0 & 1 \end{pmatrix}$, respectively, i.e., the point instances lie in vertical intervals of length 2 (Fig. 6.1(b)). In this scenario, the location uncertainties of $s_1(q), s_2(q), s_3(q)$ are independent, s_4 will be inside the circle they define (Fig. 6.1(c)). Now, let the parametric uncertainty model $(q, \bar{q}, \Delta)$ be defined by one parameter $(k = 1)$ and a vector $q = (q_1)$, where $\Delta_1 = [-1, 1]$ and the sensitivity matrices be $A_1^T = \begin{pmatrix} 0 \\ 1 \end{pmatrix}, A_1^T = \begin{pmatrix} 0 \\ 1 \end{pmatrix}, A_1^T = \begin{pmatrix} 0 \\ 1 \end{pmatrix}$. In this scenario, the location uncertainties are dependent (coupled) so that the locations of $s_1(q), s_2(q)$ and $s_3(q)$ change in the same direction and at the same rate, and the radius of the circle they define is always 2 (Fig. 6.1(d)). Thus, s_4 will always be outside the circle regardless of the location uncertainty of $s_1(q), s_2(q), s_3(q)$. Ignoring the dependency between $s_1(q), s_2(q), s_3(q)$ leads to an incorrect classification of s_4.

A central question is determining the topological stability of a VD: Given a set of points whose locations are uncertain, determine if the VD structure is the same for all possible point locations. Most previous works on VD stability focus on small point location perturbations, e.g., floating point errors and small deviations, assuming that the point location uncertainties are isotropic and independent [31, 32]. None model stability in the presence of dependencies.

Figure 6.2 illustrates Voronoi stability in the presence of independent and dependent geometric uncertainty. Let the parametric uncertainty model $(q, \bar{q}, \Delta)$ be defined by three parameters and $q = (q_1, q_2, q_3)$, where $\Delta_1 = \Delta_2 = [-1, 1], \Delta_3 = [-0.5, 0.5]$. Let $S(q) = \{s_1, s_2(q), s_3(q), s_4\}$ be a set of four points where s_1 and s_4 are exact points and $s_2(q)$ and $s_3(q)$ are uncertain points whose nominal locations are $\bar{s}_2$ and $\bar{s}_3$ (Fig. 6.2(a)). Let the sensitivity matrix of point $s_2(q)$ be $A_2^T = \begin{pmatrix} 0 & 0 & 0 \\ 1 & 0 & 0 \end{pmatrix}$, i.e., the point instances lie in a vertical interval of length 2 (Fig. 6.2(b)). Let the sensitivity matrix of point $s_3(q)$ be $A_3^T = \begin{pmatrix} 0 & 0 & 1 \\ 0 & 1 & 1 \end{pmatrix}$, i.e., the location uncertainty is a convex polygon defined by four vertices (Fig. 6.2(b)).

Notice that the location uncertainties of $s_2(q)$ and $s_3(q)$ are independent. For the nominal point instances $\bar{s}_2$ and $\bar{s}_3$, the two three-point circles defined by s_1 and $\bar{s}_2, \bar{s}_3$ and by s_4 and $\bar{s}_2, \bar{s}_3$ are centered at v_{123} and v_{234} (Fig. 6.2(c)). Since each circle does not contain s_4 and s_1, respectively, the VD consists of edges $e_{12}, e_{13}, e_{23}, e_{24}, e_{34}$. For parameter instance $q_a = (1, -1, -0.5)$,

$$s_2(q_a) = (2, 2) + (1, -1, -0.5) \begin{pmatrix} 0 & 1 \\ 0 & 0 \\ 0 & 0 \end{pmatrix} = (2, 3)$$

$$s_3(q_a) = (2, -2) + (1, -1, -0.5) \begin{pmatrix} 0 & 0 \\ 0 & 1 \\ 1 & 1 \end{pmatrix} = (1.5, -3.5)$$

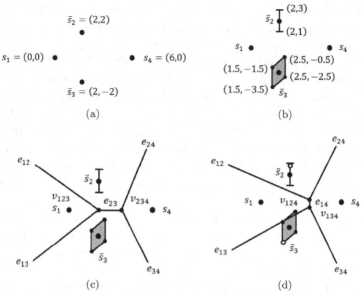

Fig. 6.2. Illustration of two VD instances of a set $S(q) = \{s_1, s_2(q), s_3(q), s_4\}$ of uncertain points: (a) points $s_1 = (0,0)$, $s_4 = (6,0)$ are exact points and points $s_2(q), s_3(q)$ are two uncertain points whose nominal locations are $\bar{s}_2 = (2,2)$ and $\bar{s}_3 = (2,-2)$ (large black dots); (b) the location uncertainty of point $s_2(q)$ is a line interval whose vertices are $(2,3)$ and $(2,1)$ (black lines); the location uncertainty of point $s_3(q)$ is a convex polygon whose vertices are $\langle(2.5,-2.5),(1.5,-3.5),(1.5,-1.5),(2.5,-0.5)\rangle$ (small black dots, black lines); the interior (gray) shows the possible locations of $s_3(q)$; (c) VD edges (black lines) $e_{12}, e_{13}, e_{23}, e_{24}, e_{34}$ and vertices $v_{123} = (2,0), v_{234} = (3.5,0)$ (small black dots) of nominal point instances $\bar{s}_2 = (2,2)$ and $\bar{s}_3 = (2,-2)$; (d) VD edges $e_{12}, e_{14}, e_{13}, e_{24}, e_{34}$ and vertices $v_{124} = (3,0.17)$ and $v_{134} = (3,-0.79)$ of point instances $s_2(q_a) = (2,3)$ and $s_3(q_a) = (1.5,-3.5)$ (white dots). Since the two VD instances have different topologies, the uncertain VD of $S(q)$ is unstable. For the dependent case, when $s_2(q_a) = (2,3)$, $s_3(q_a)$ is on the line segment whose endpoints are $(1.5,-1.5),(2.5,-0.5)$ when $s_2(q_a) = (2,2)$, $s_3(q_a)$ is on the line segment whose endpoints are $(1.5,-2.5)(2.5,-1.5)$ when $s_2(q_a) = (2,1)$, then $s_3(q_a)$ is on the line segment whose endpoints are $(1.5,-3.5)(2.5,-2.5)$. With dependencies, the uncertain VD is stable.

and the three-point circles defined by $s_1, s_2(q_a), s_4$ and by $s_1, s_3(q_a), s_4$ are centered at v_{124} and v_{134}, respectively (Fig. 6.2(d)). Since each circle does not contain $s_2(q_a)$ and $s_3(q_a)$, the VD consists of edges $e_{12}, e_{14}, e_{13}, e_{24}, e_{34}$. Note that the two VDs have different edges and vertices depending on the actual location of $s_2(q)$

and $s_3(q)$. Consequently, the VD of the independent uncertain points $S(q)$ is unstable. Now, let the parametric uncertainty model $(q, \bar{q}, \Delta)$ be defined by two parameters, $q = (q_1, q_2)$, where $\Delta_1 = [-1, 1], \Delta_2 = [-0.5, 0.5]$ and the sensitivity matrices be $A_2^T = \begin{pmatrix} 0 & 0 \\ 1 & 0 \end{pmatrix}, A_3^T = \begin{pmatrix} 0 & 1 \\ 1 & 1 \end{pmatrix}$, i.e., the location uncertainties of $s_2(q)$ and $s_3(q)$ are dependent, so that their locations change in the same direction and at the same rate. In this case, s_4 will be always outside the circle defined by $s_1, s_2(q), s_3(q)$. Thus, the VD of the dependent uncertain points $S(q)$ always consists of edges $e_{12}, e_{13}, e_{23}, e_{24}, e_{34}$ and vertices v_{123}, v_{234}, so it is topologically stable.

6.2 Voronoi Diagram and Delaunay Triangulation of LPGUM Points

We define next the uncertain VD and uncertain DT of a set of LPGUM points and their properties.

6.2.1 Definitions and properties

Let $S(q) = \{s_1(q), \ldots, s_n(q)\}$ be a set of n LPGUM points defined n sensitivity matrices, each of size $k \times 2$ $A_1, \ldots, A_2$ over parametric model $(q, \bar{q}, \Delta)$ and let $\bar{S} = \{\bar{s}_1, \ldots, \bar{s}_n\}$ be the corresponding set of nominal points.

The **uncertain VD** of $S(q)$ is

$$VD(S(q)) = (V(S(q)), E(S(q)), F(S(q)))$$

where $V(S(q)), E(S(q))$ and $F(S(q))$ are the vertices, edges and faces of the uncertain VD, respectively. The corresponding **nominal VD** is $VD(\bar{S}) = (V(\bar{S}), E(\bar{S}), F(\bar{S}))$, also denoted by $\bar{V}D = (\bar{V}, \bar{E}, \bar{F})$. An uncertain VD is **dependent** iff at least two coordinates of two or more LPGUM points depend on at least one common parameter. Otherwise, it is **independent**. Figure 6.3(a) shows an example.

An **uncertain vertex** $v_{ijl}(q) \in V(S(q))$ is defined by three LPGUM points $s_i(q), s_j(q), s_l(q)$. The corresponding nominal vertex is denoted by $\bar{v}_{ijl}$. As we will see later, $v_{ijl}(q)$ is not an LPGUM point.

An ***LPGUM bisector*** $b_{ij}(q)$ is the LPGUM line that is equidistant from two LPGUM points $s_i(q), s_j(q)$. The corresponding nominal bisector is denoted by $\bar{b}_{ij}$. The bisector $b_{ij}(q)$ is an LPGUM line (see proof in Section 6.3).

An ***uncertain edge*** $e_{ij}(q) \in E(S(q))$ is a segment of the LPGUM bisector defined by two LPGUM points $s_i(q), s_j(q)$. The nominal edge is denoted by $\bar{e}_{ij}$. As we will see later, $e_{ij}(q)$ is not an LPGUM edge.

An ***uncertain face*** $f_i(q) \in F(S(q))$ is defined by LPGUM point $s_i(q)$. The corresponding nominal face is denoted by $\bar{f}_i$. The face $f_i(q)$ is defined by its uncertain edges.

The ***uncertain Delaunay triangulation*** of $S(q)$ is

$$DT(S(q)) = (S(q), E(S(q)))$$

where $S(q)$ and $E(S(q))$ are the vertices and edges of the DT, respectively. The uncertain vertices are the points $S(q)$. The uncertain edges $e_{ij}(q) \in E(S(q))$ are the LPGUM edges defined by two LPGUM points $s_i(q), s_j(q)$. The ***nominal Delaunay triangulation*** is $DT(\bar{S}) = (\bar{S}, E(\bar{S}))$, also denoted by $\bar{DT} = (\bar{S}, \bar{E})$. An LPGUM Delaunay triangulation is ***dependent*** iff at least two coordinates of two or more LPGUM points depend on at least one common parameter. Otherwise, it is ***independent***. Note that since the vertices and edges of an uncertain DT are LPGUM, the uncertain DT is also LPGUM. Figure 6.3(b) shows an example.

The following properties hold for instances of the Voronoi vertices, edges and faces. Let $\text{dist}(s, f)$ denote the Euclidean distance between points s and f. Let p be a point in the plane.

Vertex instance $v_{ijl}(q_a)$. A point p is a vertex in the VD instance $VD(S(q))$ iff p is the center of an empty three-point circle defined by point instances $s_i(q_a), s_j(q_a), s_l(q_a)$:

$$v_{ijl}(q_a) = \left\{ \begin{array}{c} p | \text{dist}(p, s_i(q_a)) = \text{dist}(p, s_j(q_a)) \\ = \text{dist}(p, s_l(q_a)) \leq \text{dist}(p, s_m(q_a)) \\ \exists i, j, l : 1 \leq i \neq j \neq l \leq n, \forall m : 1 \leq m \leq n \end{array} \right\}$$

Edge instance $e_{ij}(q_a)$. A point p lies on edge $e_{ij}(q_a)$ iff p is the center of an empty two-point circle defined by point instances $s_i(q_a), s_j(q_a)$:

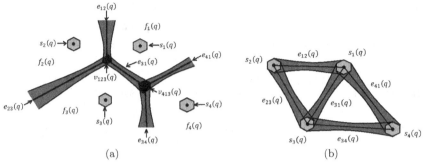

Fig. 6.3. Illustration of (a) uncertain Voronoi diagram $VD(S(q))$ of LPGUM point set $S(q) = \{s_1(q), s_2(q), s_3(q), s_4(q)\}$ (gray zonotopes). The nominal points are $\bar{s}_1, \bar{s}_2, \bar{s}_3, \bar{s}_4$ (black dots); the nominal edges are $\bar{e}_{12}, \bar{e}_{23}, \bar{e}_{31}, \bar{e}_{41}, \bar{e}_{34}$ (black segments). The uncertain vertices, edges and faces are $v_{123}(q), v_{413}(q)$ (black region), $e_{12}(q), e_{23}(q), e_{31}(q), e_{41}(q), e_{34}(q)$ (light gray) and $f_1(q), f_2(q), f_3(q), f_4(q)$; (b) corresponding uncertain Delaunay triangulation $DT(S(q))$. The nominal points are $\bar{s}_1, \bar{s}_2, \bar{s}_3, \bar{s}_4$, the nominal edges are $\bar{e}_{12}, \bar{e}_{23}, \bar{e}_{31}, \bar{e}_{41}, \bar{e}_{34}$ and the uncertain edges are $e_{12}(q), e_{23}(q), e_{31}(q), e_{41}(q), e_{34}(q)$.

$$
e_{ij}(q_a) = \left\{ \begin{array}{c} p | \mathrm{dist}(p, s_i(q_a)) = \mathrm{dist}(p, s_j(q_a)) \le \mathrm{dist}(p, s_l(q_a)) \\ \exists i, j : 1 \le i \ne j \le n, \forall l : 1 \le l \le n \end{array} \right\}
$$

Face instance $f_i(q_a)$. A point p lies in face $f_i(q_a)$ iff p is closest to point $s_i(q_a)$ out of all points in $S(q_a)$:

$$
f_i(q_a) = \{ p | \mathrm{dist}(p, s_i(q_a)) \le \mathrm{dist}(p, s_j(q_a)), \forall j \ne i : 1 \le j \le n \}
$$

6.2.2 Uncertain Voronoi diagram equivalence and stability

We define next an equivalence relation between uncertain VD and DT instances, define stability with respect to them and present an algorithm for efficiently testing it.

Definition 6.1. *Two VD instances* $VD(S(q_a))$ *and* $VD(S(q_b))$ *are* **equivalent** *iff*

1. *For each vertex* $v_{ijl}(q_a) \in V(S(q_a))$ *defined by three-point instances* $s_i(q_a), s_j(q_a), s_l(q_a) \in S(q_a)$ *in counterclockwise order, there is a corresponding vertex* $v_{ijl}(q_b) \in V(S(q_b))$ *defined by three-point instances* $s_i(q_b), s_j(q_b),$ *and* $s_l(q_b) \in S(q_b)$ *also in counterclockwise order.*

2. *For each edge $e_{ij}(q_a) \in E(S(q_a))$ defined by two-point instances $s_i(q_a), s_j(q_a) \in S(q_a)$, there is a corresponding edge $e_{ij}(q_b) \in E(S(q_b))$ defined by two-point instances $s_i(q_b), s_j(q_b) \in S(q_b)$.*

The equivalence between the faces in $F(S(q_a))$ and $F(S(q_b))$ directly follows from the two conditions above since the same LPGUM points define their face vertices and edges.

For example, in Fig. 6.2(c), in the dependent case, the nominal Voronoi diagram $\overline{VD} = (\bar{V}, \bar{E}, \bar{F})$ and the VD instance $VD(S(q_a)) = (V(S(q_a)), E(S(q_a)), F(S(q_a)))$ for $q_a = (-1, -0.5)$ are equivalent since (1) $\bar{V} = \{v_{123}, v_{234}\}$ and $V(S(q_a)) = \{v_{123}(q_a), v_{234}(q_a)\}$, and (2) $\bar{E} = \{\bar{e}_{12}, \bar{e}_{13}, \bar{e}_{23}, \bar{e}_{24}, \bar{e}_{34}\}$ and $E(q_a) = \{e_{12}(q_a), e_{13}(q_a), e_{23}(q_a), e_{24}(q_a), e_{34}(q_a)\}$ are equivalent.

Definition 6.2. *Two Delaunay triangulation instances* DT $(S(q_a)), DT(S(q_b))$ *are* equivalent *iff for each triangle $e_{ij}(q_a)$, $e_{jl}(q_a), e_{li}(q_a) \in E(S(q_a))$ defined by three-point instances $s_i(q_a), s_j(q_a), s_l(q_a) \in S(q_a)$ in counterclockwise order there is a corresponding triangle $e_{ij}(q_b), e_{jl}(q_b), e_{li}(q_b) \in E(S(q_b))$ defined by three-point instances $s_i(q_b), s_j(q_b), s_l(q_b) \in S(q_b)$ in counterclockwise order.*

Definition 6.3. *An* uncertain Voronoi diagram *$VD(S(q))$ is* stable *iff for every parameter vector instance $q_a \in \Delta$, all VD instances $VD(S(q_a))$ are equivalent to the nominal location of Voronoi diagram $\overline{VD}$.*

For example, in Fig. 6.2, the VD in $VD(S(q))$ is unstable for the independent case (Fig. 6.2(c)) and stable for the dependent case (Fig. 6.2(d)).

Definition 6.4. *An* uncertain Delaunay triangulation *DT $(S(q))$ is* stable *iff for every parameter vector instance $q_a \in \Delta$, all Delaunay triangulation instances $DT(S(q_a))$ are equivalent to the nominal location of Delaunay triangulation $\overline{DT}$.*

Similar concepts can be defined for the **uncertain CH**. Let $CH(S(q)) = \langle s_{i1}(q), \ldots, s_{im}(q) \rangle$ be the uncertain CH of LPGUM point set $S(q)$ defined by boundary points $s_{ij}(q)$ and let $CH(S(q_a)) = \langle s_{i1}(q_a), \ldots, s_{im}(q_a) \rangle$ be a **CH instance** for $q_a \in \Delta$ where $s_{i1}(q_a), \ldots, s_{im}(q_a)$ are the boundary point instances.

Definition 6.5. *Two CH instances* $CH(S(q_a)) = \langle s_{i1}(q_a), \ldots,$ $s_{im}(q_a)\rangle$ *and* $CH(S(q_b)) = \langle s_{j1}(q_b), \ldots, s_{jn}(q_b)\rangle$ *are equivalent iff their number of points is equal,* $m = n$ *and there is a one-to-one correspondence between their boundary points,* $s_{i1}(q) = s_{jd}(q), \ldots, s_{im}(q) = s_{j(d+m-1)}(q)$ *where* $1 \leq d \leq n$ *and* $d + l$ *is the* l^{th} *point in counterclockwise order after d.*

Definition 6.6. *An* **uncertain convex hull** $CH(S(q))$ *is* **stable** *iff for every* $q_a \in \Delta$, *all CH instances* $CH(S(q_a))$ *are equivalent to the nominal location of convex hull* $\bar{CH}$.

We now show that when an uncertain VD is unstable, it may have an exponential number of non-equivalent VD instances. This is an undesirable situation, since computations on an unstable uncertain VD may also require exponential time. We first prove a Lemma about unstable CHs and use it to prove the uncertain VD result.

Lemma 6.1. *When the uncertain convex hull* $CH(S(q))$ *is not stable, there may be an exponential number of non-equivalent CH instances.*

Proof. By construction of an example that has an exponential number of non-equivalent CH instances (Fig. 6.4), let p_1, p_2, p_3, p_4 be four points on the unit circle (radius of 1 unit) centered at the origin; let $S(q) = \{s_1(q), \ldots, s_n(q)\}$ be a set of $n > 4$ LPGUM points whose nominal locations are evenly distributed on the unit circle in counterclockwise order. Let $q = (q_1, \ldots, q_n)$ be an n-parameter vector. For each LPGUM point $s_i(q)$, we define an angle $t_i = \frac{2\pi}{n}i$, so that the nominal point location is $\bar{s}_i = (\cos t_i, \sin t_i)$. We define the uncertainty domain $\Delta_i = [-1/2, 1/2]$ and the $k \times 2$ sensitivity matrix $A_i^T = \begin{pmatrix} 0 & \cdots & 0 & 1 & 0 & \cdots & 0 \\ 0 & \cdots & 0 & \tan t_i & 0 & \cdots & 0 \end{pmatrix}$ such that all the columns are zero except the column $(A_i)_{*,i}^T = \begin{pmatrix} 1 \\ \tan t_i \end{pmatrix}$. The uncertainty domain and the sensitivity matrices are defined so that there exists a parameter vector instance q_α such that point instances $s_i(q_\alpha)$ can lie inside or outside the square formed by points p_1, p_2, p_3, p_4. In particular, all points are inside for $q_i = 1/2$ when point $\bar{s}_i$ lies in the first or in the four quadrants, otherwise inside for $q_i = -1/2$. For this parameter vector instance q_α, $CH(S(q_\alpha)) = \langle p_1, p_2, p_3, p_4\rangle$.

Note that for $\bar{q} = 0$, the LPGUM points $\bar{s}_1, \ldots, \bar{s}_n$ lie on the unit circle, so $\overline{CH} = \langle p_1, p_2, p_3, p_4, \bar{s}_1, \ldots, \bar{s}_n \rangle$.

By construction, each LPGUM point $s_i(q)$ depends on a single parameter q_i. Therefore, we can choose any subset of parameters q_i and set them to $1/2$ or to $-1/2$ according to the quadrants where $s_i(q)$ lies, and set the remaining ones to 0 — this will include/exclude them from the CH. Since there are 2^n subsets, there are 2^n non-equivalent CH instances. $\quad\square$

Theorem 6.1. *An unstable uncertain Voronoi diagram $VD(S(q))$ may have an exponential number of non-equivalent VD instances.*

Proof. For the independent case, consider the uncertain VD of the set of LPGUM points in Fig. 6.4 and Lemma 6.1. The Voronoi points of the unbounded VD cells form an unstable uncertain CH with an exponential number of non-equivalent instances. Consequently, the uncertain VD has an exponential number of non-equivalent instances.

For the dependent case, let c be a constant such that $n/c = \Omega(n)$. Now, suppose that points $s_1(q), \ldots, s_c(q)$ (without loss of generality, suppose that $s_1(q), \ldots, s_c(q)$ lie in the same quadrant) all depend on parameter q_1, that points $s_{c+1}(q), \ldots, s_{2c}(q)$ depend on parameter q_2 and so on, up to points $s_{\lfloor n/c \rfloor + 1}(q), \ldots, s_n(q)$ (we assume that all the points in each sub-set lie in the same quadrant), all of which depend

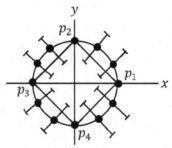

Fig. 6.4.   Illustration of the construction of a set of points on the unit circle: points $p_1 = (1, 0), p_2 = (0, 1), p_3 = (-1, 0), p_4 = (0, -1)$ and nominal locations of n LPGUM points $S(q) = \{s_1(q), \ldots, s_n(q)\}$ whose nominal locations are evenly distributed on the unit circle centered at the origin. Each LPGUM point depends on one parameter so that its uncertainty zone is a line segment that is perpendicular to the tangent of the circle at the nominal point.

on parameter $q_{\lfloor n/c \rfloor}$. Consequently, there are $2^{\lfloor n/c \rfloor}$ non-equivalent VD instances. □

We now investigate how to test if an uncertain VD is stable.

Theorem 6.2. *An uncertain Voronoi diagram $VD(S(q))$ is stable iff all LPGUM in-circle tests on the circles defined by the vertices $V(S(q))$ of $VD(S(q))$ are negative, i.e., every LPGUM point $s_m(q)$ is outside the LPGUM three-point circle $c_{ijl}(q) = circle(s_i(q), s_j(q), s_l(q))$ that defines vertex $v_{ijl}(q) \in V(S(q))$.*

Figure 6.5 shows an example of a positive LPGUM in-circle test.

Proof. ⟹ Assume by contradiction that uncertain Voronoi diagram $VD(S(q))$ is stable and that there exists a circle $c_{ijl}(q) = circle(s_i(q), s_j(q), s_l(q))$ that defines a vertex $v_{ijl}(q) \in V(S(q))$ for which the LPGUM in-circle test for $s_m(q)$ is positive. This means that $\exists q_a \in \Delta$ for which point instance $s_m(q_a)$ is inside circle instance $c_{ijl}(q_a)$.

For the circle $c_{ijl}(q)$ that defines vertex $v_{ijl}(q)$, $\exists q_b \in \Delta$ such that circle $c_{ijl}(q_b) = circle(s_i(q_b), s_j(q_b), s_l(q_b))$ is empty, so $v_{ijl}(q_b) \in V(S(q_b))$. However, the circle $c_{ijl}(q_a) = circle(s_i(q_a), s_j(q_a), s_l(q_a))$ cannot define a vertex $v_{ijl}(q_a) \in V(S(q_a))$ because it contains the point $s_m(q_a)$. Consequently, $VD(S(q_a)) \neq VD(S(q_b))$ and thus $VD(S(q))$ is not stable.

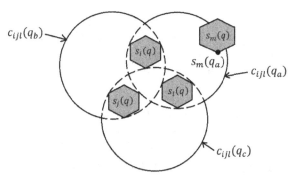

Fig. 6.5.   Example of an LPGUM circle $c_{ijl}(q)$ for which the in-circle test for point $s_m(q)$ is positive. In gray are LPGUM points $s_i(q), s_j(q), s_l(q), s_m(q)$. In black are circle instances $c_{ijl}(q_a), c_{ijl}(q_b), c_{ijl}(q_c)$. The black continuous line is the outer envelope of circle $c_{ijl}(q)$. Point instance $s_m(q_a)$ is inside circle instance $c_{ijl}(q_a)$ and outside circle instances $c_{ijl}(q_b), c_{ijl}(q_c)$.

$\Longleftarrow$ Every circle $\bar{c}_{ijl} = circle(\bar{s}_i, \bar{s}_j, \bar{s}_l)$ that defines a vertex $\bar{v}_{ijl} \in \bar{V}$ in $\overline{VD}$ is by definition an empty circle. When all in-circle tests are negative, the circle $c_{ijl}(q_a) = circle(s_i(q_a), s_j(q_a), s_l(q_a))$ is empty for all parameter vector instances q_a. Therefore, vertex $v_{ijl}(q_a) \in V(S(q_a))$. Consequently, for all q_a, the VD instance $VD(S(q_a))$ has the same vertices defined by the same three points as those of $\overline{VD}$. Similarly, it has the same edges, as the vertices are common intersections of three bisectors, and the same faces. Therefore, $\forall q_a \in \Delta, VD(S(q_a)) = \overline{VD}$, and so $VD(S(q))$ is stable. $\qquad\square$

Theorem 6.3. *An uncertain Voronoi diagram $VD(S(q))$ is stable iff $DT(S(q))$ is stable.*

Proof. $\Longrightarrow$ $VD(S(q))$ is stable iff all LPGUM in-circle tests on the circles that define the vertices $V(S(q))$ of $VD(S(q))$ are negative, i.e., every LPGUM point $s_m(q) \in S(q)$ is outside the LPGUM three-point circle $c_{ijl}(q)$ that defines vertex $v_{ijl}(q) \in V(S(q))$. When every LPGUM point $s_m(q)$ is outside $c_{ijl}(q)$ then for every parameter instance $q_a \in \Delta$, the point instances $s_i(q_a), s_j(q_a), s_l(q_a)$ define the Delaunay triangle $e_{ij}(q_a), e_{jl}(q_a), e_{li}(q_a) \in E(S(q_a))$.

$\Longleftarrow$ $DT(S(q))$ is stable iff for every $q_a \in \Delta$, all Delaunay triangulation instances $DT(S(q_a))$ are equivalent to the nominal location of Delaunay triangulation $\overline{DT}$, i.e., if $\bar{s}_i, \bar{s}_j, \bar{s}_l$ define Delaunay triangle $\bar{e}_{ij}, \bar{e}_{jl}, \bar{e}_{li}$ then for every parameter instance $q_a \in \Delta$, the point instances $s_i(q_a), s_j(q_a), s_l(q_a)$ define the Delaunay triangle $e_{ij}(q_a), e_{jl}(q_a), e_{li}(q_a)$. Therefore, by the definition of the Delaunay triangulation, every LPGUM point $s_m(q)$ is outside the LPGUM three-point circle $c_{ijl}(q)$. Thus, all the LPGUM in-circle tests on the circles defined by the vertices $V(S(q))$ of $VD(S(q))$ are negative. $\qquad\square$

Theorem 6.4. *To determine if an uncertain Voronoi diagram $VD(S(q))$ is stable, it suffices to perform an LPGUM in-circle test on the LPGUM three-point circles defined by its vertices $V(S(q))$. The time complexity of the in-circle test is $O(nP_4(k))$, where $P_4(k)$ is the complexity of quartic k-variable optimization when the nominal Voronoi diagram $\overline{VD}$ is given.*

Proof. The in-circle test determines if LPGUM point $r(q)$ is outside LPGUM three-point circle $c_{uvw}(q) = circle(u(q), v(q), w(q))$, i.e., iff for every instance of the parameter vector $q_a \in \Delta$, point instance $r(q_a)$ is outside circle $c_{uvw}(q_a)$. The location of point $r(q)$ with respect circle $c_{uvw}(q)$ is determined by the sign of the determinant:

$$\begin{vmatrix} d_{ux}(q) & d_{uy}(q) & (d_{ux}(q))^2+(d_{uy}(q))^2 & 1 \\ d_{vx}(q) & d_{vy}(q) & (d_{vx}(q))^2+(d_{vy}(q))^2 & 1 \\ d_{wx}(q) & d_{wy}(q) & (d_{wx}(q))^2+(d_{wy}(q))^2 & 1 \\ d_{rx}(q) & d_{ry}(q) & (d_{rx}(q))^2+(d_{ry}(q))^2 & 1 \end{vmatrix}$$

The determinant is positive for a parameter vector instance q_a for which point $r(q_a)$ is inside $c_{uvw}(q_a)$. It is negative for a q_a for which $r(q_a)$ is outside $c_{uvw}(q_a)$. It is zero for a parameter vector instance for which point instances $u(q_a), v(q_a), w(q_a), r(q_a)$ are co-circular. The determinant yields a multivariate quartic programming problem with interval constraints that can be solved in $p_4(q)$ time, where $p_4(q)$ is the complexity of quartic k-variable optimization.

In its general form, solving the quartic multivariate sign problem with interval constraints is known to be NP-hard in the number of variables [75]. However, in practice, individual point locations depend on only a few (<10) parameters and the actual number of dependent (coupled) parameters m is also usually small, and much smaller than the total number of parameters, $m \ll k$. In these cases, the bounded quartic linear optimization problems depend on m and not on k, which makes solving them practical. Also, note that this is the worst-case complexity: recent papers indicate that the average case performance may be lower [76]. Finally, approximation algorithms allow for efficient solving to any desired accuracy, e.g., semi-definite relaxation techniques with a guaranteed approximation ratio of $1 - O(k^2)$ [76].

A single LPGUM in-circle test takes $O(P_4(k))$ time and there are $O(n)$ triangles in the $DT(S(q))$. For any two adjacent triangles, $s_a(q), s_b(q), s_c(q)$ and $s_a(q), s_b(q), s_d(q)$, check that $s_d(q)$ is outside the circle $c_{abc}(q) = \text{circle}(s_a(q), s_b(q), s_c(q))$ and $s_c(q)$ is outside the circle $c_{abd}(q) = \text{circle}(s_a(q), s_b(q), s_d(q))$. Each triangle has three adjacent triangles. Consequently, there are $O(n)$ in-circle tests in total, and the overall time complexity of stability testing is $O(nP_4(k))$. $\square$

Theorem 6.5. *For the independent case, the expected complexity of testing the stability of an uncertain Voronoi diagram $VD(S(q))$ is $O(nk \log k)$.*

Proof.   An efficient in-circle test algorithm for the independent case is as follows. First, we compute the outer envelope of LPGUM circle $c_{abc}(q)$ with the algorithm described in Section 3.3.3. Next, for each edge on the uncertainty envelope of query point $d(q)$, we test that the uncertainty envelope does not intersect the three circles that define the outer envelope and that its endpoints are outside those circles. The expected time complexity of the independent in-circle test is $O(k \log k)$: computing the three circles, the outer envelope requires $O(k \log k)$ expected time. Testing each zonotope edge and its endpoints requires $O(k)$ time since there are $O(k)$ such edges. The overall expected time complexity of the in-circle test is thus $O(nk \log k)$.   □

6.3   LPGUM Bisectors

We define next the LPGUM bisector.

Theorem 6.6. *An LPGUM bisector $b_{12}(q)$ equidistant from two LPGUM points $s_1(q), s_2(q)$ is an LPGUM line.*

Figure 6.6 shows an example of an LPGUM bisector defined by two LPGUM points.

Proof.   Let $s_1(q), s_2(q) \in S(q)$ be two LPGUM points. Then,

$$s_1(q) = \bar{s}_1 + qA_1$$
$$s_2(q) = \bar{s}_2 + qA_2$$

Let $\vec{u}_{12}(q)$ be the LPGUM vector defined by these two LPGUM points, $\vec{u}_{12}(q) = \bar{s}_2 - \bar{s}_1 + q(A_2 - A_1)$; let $\vec{u}_{12} = \bar{s}_2 - \bar{s}_1$ and $A_{u12} = A_2 - A_1$. Then,

$$\vec{u}_{12}(q) = \vec{u}_{12} + qA_{u12} = (\bar{d}_{12x} + q(A_{u12})_{*,x}, \bar{d}_{12y} + q(A_{u12})_{*,y})$$

Denote by $\vec{u}_{12}^{\perp}(q)$ the vector perpendicular to vector $\vec{u}_{12}(q)$:

$$\vec{u}_{12}^{\perp}(q) = (-\bar{d}_{12y} + q(-1((A_{u12})_{*,y})), \bar{d}_{12x} + q(A_{u12})_{*,x})$$

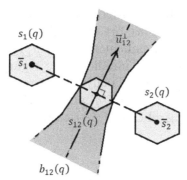

Fig. 6.6. Example of an LPGUM bisector $b_{12}(q)$ equidistant from LPGUM points $s_1(q) = \bar{s}_1 + qA_1$ and $s_2(q) = \bar{s}_2 + qA_2$. The LPGUM bisector is an LPGUM line defined by LPGUM vector $\vec{u}_{12}^{\perp}(q)$ and LPGUM point $s_{12}(q)$. LPGUM vector $\vec{u}_{12}^{\perp}(q)$ is vertical to the LPGUM vector defined by points $s_1(q), s_2(q)$. Point $s_{12}(q)$ lies in the middle of the uncertain segment defined by points $s_1(q), s_2(q)$.

Let $\vec{u}_{12}^{\perp} = (-\bar{d}_{12y}, \bar{d}_{12x})$ and $A_{\vec{u}_{12}^{\perp}} = (-1((A_{u12})_{*,y}), (A_{u12})_{*,x})$. Then,

$$\vec{u}_{12}^{\perp}(q) = \vec{u}_{12}^{\perp} + qA_{\vec{u}_{12}^{\perp}}$$

LPGUM point $s_{12}(q)$ is equidistant from the LPGUM lines defined by $s_1(q)$ and $s_2(q)$:

$$s_{12}(q) = \frac{1}{2}(s_1(q) + s_2(q))$$

Let $\bar{s}_{12} = \frac{1}{2}(\bar{d}_{1x} + \bar{d}_{2x}, \bar{d}_{1y} + \bar{d}_{2y})$ and $A_{s_{12}} = \frac{1}{2}(A_1 + A_2)$. Then,

$$s_{12}(q) = \bar{s}_{12} + qA_{s_{12}}$$

The bisector of LPGUM points $s_1(q)$ and $s_2(q)$ is the LPGUM line $b_{12}(q)$:

$$b_{12}(q) = s_{12}(q) + \alpha(\vec{u}_{12}^{\perp}(q)), \quad \alpha \in \mathbb{R}$$

Note that the uncertain zone of bisector $b_{12}(q)$ may intersect the uncertain zones of points $s_1(q)$ and $s_2(q)$. $\qquad\square$

Lemma 6.2. *The computation of all LPGUM bisectors of a stable uncertain VD requires $O(nk^2)$ time when the nominal VD is given.*

Proof. Given two LPGUM points $s_1(q), s_2(q) \in S(q)$, compute first the LPGUM vector $\vec{u}_{12}(q)$ that passes through these points. Next, compute the perpendicular vector $\vec{u}_{12}^{\perp}(q)$ and the LPGUM point $s_{12}(q)$ that lies in the middle of the segment defined by $s_1(q)$ and $s_2(q)$ in constant time. Finally, compute the LPGUM bisector line defined by LPGUM vector $\vec{u}(q)$ and LPGUM point $s(q)$ in $O(k^2)$ time. Thus, computing all LPGUM bisectors in the VD takes $O(nk^2)$ time. □

6.4   Intersection of Two Independent LPGUM Lines

We first define the intersection between an LPGUM line and an exact line and use it as a basis to define the intersection between two LPGUM lines.

Definition 6.7. *Let $h_1 = a_1 x + b_1, h_2 = a_2 x + b_2$ be two lines. Line h_1 is said to be **decreasing** with respect to line h_2 iff $a_1 < a_2$. Line h_1 is said to be increasing with respect to line h_2 iff $a_1 > a_2$.*

Lemma 6.3. *Let h be an exact line and let $l(q)$ be an LPGUM line such that $h \neq l(q_a), \forall q_a \in \Delta$. Then either*

1. *h intersects the upper or the lower envelope of LPGUM line $l(q)$ twice iff there exists a line instance $l(q_b), q_b \in \Delta$ that is parallel to line h;*
2. *h intersects the upper and lower envelopes of LPGUM line $l(q)$ no more than once.*

Figure 6.7 illustrates these cases.

Proof. Assume first that line h is contained in line $l(q)$. In this case, $\exists q_a \in \Delta$ such that $l(q_a) = h$, that is, line h and line instance $l(q_a)$ are parallel, so line h does not intersect with the envelope of line $l(q)$. Now, assume line h is not contained in line $l(q)$ and, without loss of generality, assume that line h is above the lower envelope of $l(q)$. Since the upper envelope of $l(q)$ is a monotonic convex envelope chain with respect to the nominal line $\bar{l}$, the line h and the upper envelope of line $l(q)$ intersect at one or two points (Fig. 6.7).

When line h and the upper envelope of line $l(q)$ intersect at one point (Fig. 6.7(a)), then, due to the convexity and monotonicity of

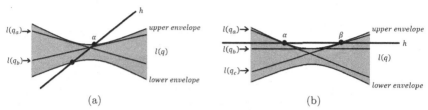

Fig. 6.7. Intersection between an LPGUM line $l(q)$ and exact line h: (a) intersection between the upper envelope of line $l(q)$ and line h is point α, the sign of the vector of line h does not change with respect to every instance of line $l(q_a), \forall q_a \in \Delta$; (b) the intersections between the upper envelope of line $l(q)$ and line h are points α and β. The slope of line instance $l(q_a), q_a \in \Delta$ decreases with respect to line h, line h is parallel to line instance $l(q_b), q_b \in \Delta$. The slope of line instance $l(q_c), q_c \in \Delta$ increases with respect to line h.

the envelope, the sign of the vector of line h does not change with respect to every line instance $l(q_a), \forall q_a \in \Delta$. In this case, $\nexists q_b$ such that line h is parallel to line instance $l(q_b)$.

When line h and the upper envelope of line $l(q)$ intersect at two points (Fig. 6.7(b)), then, due to the convexity and monotonicity of the envelope, the sign of the vector of line h changes with respect to line instance $l(q_a)$. Without loss of generality, assume that the nominal line $\bar{l}$ is parallel to axis x. Let α and β be the intersection points of the line h and the upper envelope of line $l(q)$. Let $l(q_a)$ be a line instance that is tangent to the upper envelope at a point to the left of α.

Due to the convexity of the envelope, the slope of line $l(q_a)$ decreases with respect to line h (Fig. 6.7(b)). Similarly, let $l(q_c)$ be a line instance such that $l(q_c)$ is tangent to upper envelope at a point to the right of β. Due to the convexity of the envelope, the slope of line $l(q_c)$ increases with respect to line h. Thus, when the line h and the upper envelope of line $l(q)$ intersect at two points, due continuity and monotonicity, there exists a line instance $l(q_b), q_b \in \Delta$ that is parallel to line h.

Notice that due to the convexity of the envelope of LPGUM line $l(q)$, every intersection between line h and line instance $l(q_a)$ occurs to the left of point α or to the right of point β and no intersection occurs between points α and β. ☐

Lemma 6.4. *Let $l(q)$ and $l'(q)$ be two LPGUM lines. If there are no line instances $l(q_c), l'(q_d)$ for $q_c, q_d \in \Delta$ such that $l(q_c)$ and $l'(q_d)$ are*

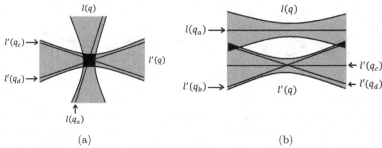

(a)   (b)

Fig. 6.8.   Intersection of two LPGUM lines $l(q)$ and $l'(q)$ (black region): (a) Case 1: the sign of the vector of line instance $l(q_a)$ does not change with respect to line instances $l'(q_c), l'(q_d)$ for $q_c, q_d \in \Delta$. For all $q_b \in \Delta$, the sign of the vector of line instance $l(q_a)$ does not change with respect to line instance $l'(q_b)$; (b) Case 2: the slope of line instance $l'(q_b), q_b \in \Delta$ increases with respect to line instance $l(q_a)$. Line instance $l'(q_c), q_c \in \Delta$ is parallel to line instance $l(q_a)$. The slope of line instance $l'(q_d), q_d \in \Delta$ decreases with respect to line $l(q_a)$.

parallel, then the intersection between LPGUM lines $l(q)$ and $l'(q)$ forms a single connected region.

Figure 6.8 illustrates this situation.

Proof.   Let $l(q) = u(q) + \alpha(\vec{v}(q)), \alpha \in \mathbb{R}$ and $l'(q) = u'(q) + \alpha'(\vec{v}'(q)), \alpha' \in \mathbb{R}$. The envelope of LPGUM line $l(q)$ consists of two monotonic chains with respect to nominal line $\bar{l}$.

When the sign of every vector instance $\vec{v}(q_a)$ of line $l(q)$ does not change with respect to every vector instance $\vec{v}'(q_b)$ of line $l'(q)$, then due to the convexity and monotonicity of the LPGUM line envelopes, $\nexists q_c, q_d$ such that line instances $l(q_c), l'(q_d)$ are parallel (Fig. 6.8(a)). Therefore, by Lemma 6.3, every line instance $l(q_a)$ intersects the envelope of line $l'(q)$ only once. Consequently, the intersection between LPGUM lines $l(q)$, $l'(q)$ consists of a single connected region.

When the sign of at least one vector instance $\vec{v}(q_a)$ of line $l(q)$ changes with respect to a vector instance $\vec{v}'(q_b)$ of line $l'(q)$, then due to the continuity and monotonicity of the LPGUM line, there exists a line instance $l(q_c)$ that is parallel to line instance $l'(q_b)$ (Fig. 6.8(b)). In this case, by Lemma 6.3, line instance $l'(q_b)$ intersects with the upper or lower envelopes of line $l(q)$ more than once. Consequently, the intersection between LPGUM lines $l(q)l'(q)$ consists of two regions.   □

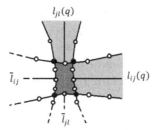

Fig. 6.9. Illustration of the intersection between two LPGUM bisectors $l_{ij}(q), l_{jl}(q)$ of an independent uncertain VD forming a pseudo-square (dark gray region) in which each "edge" is a chain. Black points are the intersections between the envelopes of lines $l_{ij}(q), l_{jl}(q)$ and white points are the endpoints of the chains.

6.5 Properties of an Independent Uncertain Voronoi Diagram Vertex

In this section, we first define the common intersection of two LPGUM bisectors. Next, we define the intersection of three LPGUM bisectors and of the resulting uncertain VD vertex.

Definition 6.8. *A **pseudo-square** is defined by four points in convex position, connected by a concave chain.*

Figure 6.9 shows an example of a pseudo-square.

Definition 6.9. *A **pseudo-polygon** is defined by at least three points in convex position, connected by a concave chain.*

Lemma 6.5. *The common intersection of two independent LPGUM bisectors is a pseudo-square whose edges are chains.*

Figure 6.9 illustrates this situation.

Proof. Let $VD(S(q))$ be an uncertain VD and let $l_{ij}(q), l_{jl}(q), l_{li}(q)$ be the three LPGUM bisectors that define the uncertain Voronoi vertex $v_{ijl}(q) \in V(S(q))$. In a stable uncertain Voronoi diagram $VD(S(q))$, all bisector instances $l_{ij}(q_a), l_{jl}(q_a), l_{li}(q_a)$ intersect for $\forall q_a \in \Delta$.

The upper envelope of bisector $l_{ij}(q)$ intersects with the upper and the lower envelope of bisector $l_{jl}(q)$, for otherwise there exists a line instance $l_{ij}(q_a)$ which does not intersect with $l_{jl}(q_b)$. This contradicts the stability of the VD. The same argument holds for the intersection of the lower envelope of bisector $l_{ij}(q)$ with the upper and the lower envelopes of bisector $l_{jl}(q)$.

Consider now the intersection between LPGUM bisectors $l_{ij}(q)$ and $l_{jl}(q)$. Since we assume that all points are in a general position, for each point set instance $S(q_a), \forall q_a \in \Delta$, no three points are collinear. Thus, $\nexists q_b, q_c \in \Delta$ for which bisector instances $l_{ij}(q_b), l_{jl}(q_c)$ are parallel (Fig. 6.8(b)). Therefore, the upper and lower envelopes of bisector $l_{ij}(q)$ intersect only once with the upper and lower envelopes of bisector $l_{jl}(q)$. In this case, the intersection between LPGUM bisectors $l_{ij}(q), l_{jl}(q)$ consists of a single region, a pseudo-square, whose edges are chains (Fig. 6.9). □

Lemma 6.6. *The vertex of an independent uncertain VD is a pseudo-polygon defined by at most six convex chains.*

Proof.   The vertices of an independent uncertain VD are defined by the intersection of three LPGUM bisectors. Note that the intersection does not yield an LPGUM point. As noted in Section 2.5, the outer envelope of an independent three-point LPGUM circle is bounded by three arc segments. Thus, every vertex $v_{ijl}(q)$ of a stable uncertain VD is bounded.

Let $l_{ij}(q), l_{jl}(q), l_{li}(q)$ be the three LPGUM bisectors that define the uncertain VD vertex $v_{ijl}(q)$. The common intersection of two LPGUM bisectors $l_{ij}(q), l_{jl}(q)$ forms a pseudo-square. When a third LPGUM bisector $l_{li}(q)$ is added to the intersection, one of five cases occurs (Fig. 6.10):

1. The pseudo-square is contained in the uncertainty zone of $l_{li}(q)$.
2. One vertex of the pseudo-square is outside the intersection.
3. Two vertices of the pseudo-square are outside the intersection.
4. Three vertices of the pseudo-square are outside the intersection.
5. Four vertices of the pseudo-square are outside the intersection.

In all these cases, the intersection is a pseudo-polygon with at most six chains as its edges. □

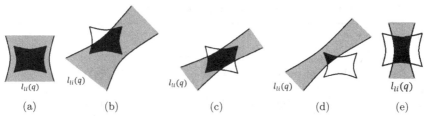

$l_{li}(q)$ $l_{li}(q)$ $l_{li}(q)$ $l_{li}(q)$ $l_{li}(q)$

(a)   (b)   (c)   (d)   (e)

Fig. 6.10. Illustration of the five cases of the intersection (black region) between the pseudo-square of two LPGUM bisectors and a third LPGUM bisector $l_{li}(q)$ (in gray): (a) the pseudo-square is fully contained inside the LPGUM line $l_{li}(q)$; (b) one vertex of the pseudo-square is outside the intersection; (c) two vertices of the pseudo-square are outside the intersection; (d) three vertices of the pseudo-square are outside the intersection; (e) four vertices of the pseudo-square are outside the intersection.

6.6 Stable Uncertain Voronoi Diagram Construction

We describe first an algorithm for computing a stable uncertain VD of a set of LPGUM points for both the independent and dependent cases. Next, we describe algorithms for the construction of vertices, edges and faces for the independent case based on the computation and intersection of LPGUM bisectors.

6.6.1 Algorithm

Table 6.1 lists the algorithm to compute a stable uncertain VD for the independent and dependent cases. First, the nominal VD is computed and tested for stability. Then, the LPGUM bisectors of every pair of neighboring points in the nominal VD are computed. Finally, the vertices, edges and faces of the uncertain VD are computed. Section 6.3 presents an algorithm for computing LPGUM bisectors for the dependent and independent cases.

The algorithm correctness follows directly from the properties of the nominal VD construction, which is the same for all the equivalent VD instances when the uncertain VD is stable.

The algorithm complexity is determined by the complexity of the stability test and the vertices, edges and faces' computation. For the dependent case, the stability test takes $O(nP_4(k))$ when the nominal VD is given; computing an LPGUM bisector takes $O(k^2)$ time (Section 6.3), so step 3 requires $O(nk^2)$ time. The uncertain dependent

Table 6.1.   Algorithm for computing a stable uncertain VD.

Input: A set of LPGUM points $S(q)$.

1. Compute the nominal Voronoi diagram $\overline{VD} = (\overline{V}, \overline{D}, \overline{E})$.
2. Test the stability of the uncertain Voronoi diagram $VD(S(q))$.
3. **If** unstable, **then** return *UNSTABLE*.
4. Compute the Voronoi diagram LPGUM bisectors of every pair of neighboring points in the nominal Voronoi diagram. Each LPGUM bisector corresponds to a nominal edge.
5. Compute the uncertain vertices $V(S(q))$ from the intersection of the three LPGUM bisectors defined by their corresponding nominal edges. Each uncertain vertex corresponds to a nominal vertex.
6. Define the Voronoi diagram edges $E(S(q))$ to be the LPGUM bisectors and uncertain vertices.
7. Define the uncertain faces $F(S(q))$ to be the uncertain vertices and uncertain edges.

Output: The uncertain Voronoi diagram $VD(S(q)) = (V(S(q)), E(S(q)), F(S(q)))$.

---

vertex computation remains an open problem. For the independent case, we have the following result.

Theorem 6.7. *The complexity of computing an independent stable uncertain VD with the algorithm listed in Table 6.1 is $O(nk^2 + n\log n)$ time and $O(nk)$ space when the nominal VD is given.*

Proof. The computation of the nominal VD in step 1 requires $O(n\log n)$ time. The stability test for an uncertain VD in step 2 takes expected $O(nk\log k)$ time for the independent case. Computing an LPGUM bisector takes $O(k^2)$ time, so step 3 requires $O(nk^2)$ time since there are $O(n)$ LPGUM bisectors. Computing an uncertain independent vertex once the LPGUM bisectors have been computed requires $O(k)$ time (Sections 6.4 and 6.5), and thus $O(nk)$ time for all $O(n)$ vertices. Overall, the computation requires $O(nk^2 + n\log n)$ time and $O(nk)$ space. $\qquad\square$

We describe next algorithms for the construction of vertices, edges and faces for the independent case. We assume that the VD is stable and that the nominal VD has been computed.

6.6.2 Uncertain Voronoi vertex computation

In the independent case, a VD vertex is defined by the intersection of three bisectors (general position).

Lemma 6.7. *The vertices of a stable uncertain VD do not intersect.*

Proof. Every vertex $v_{ijl}(q) \in V(S(q))$ of a stable uncertain Voronoi diagram $VD(S(q))$ is the center of an empty LPGUM three-point circle defined by LPGUM points $s_i(q), s_j(q), s_l(q) \in S(q)$ and does not contain any other LPGUM points. Assume by contradiction that two uncertain vertices of the uncertain VD intersect. Let $v_{ijl}(q), v_{\alpha\beta\gamma}(q) \in V(S(q))$ be the uncertain vertices of LPGUM points $s_i(q), s_j(q), s_l(q), s_\alpha(q), s_\beta(q)$ and $s_\gamma(q)$, $\{i,j,l\} \neq \{\alpha,\beta,\gamma\}$. Let $v(q_a), q_a \in \Delta$ be a vertex instance inside the intersection of uncertain vertices $v_{ijl}(q)$ and $v_{\alpha\beta\gamma}(q)$. Vertex instance $v(q_a)$ is the center of an empty circle defined by point instances $s_i(q_a), s_j(q_a), s_l(q_a)$ and also the center of an empty circle defined by point instances $s_\alpha(q_a), s_\beta(q_a), s_\gamma(q_a)$. Since both circles are empty, neither of them contains the other one, thus all the points are co-circular. This is a contradiction of the assumption than no four points are co-circular.☐

Lemma 6.8. *The complexity of a stable independent uncertain VD vertex is $O(k)$ and $O(nk)$ for all n vertices. The vertices can be computed in $O(nk)$ time when the nominal VD and its LPGUM bisectors are given.*

Proof. The complexity of an LPGUM bisector envelope is $O(k)$, as it consists of two segment chains, each of complexity $O(k)$. Since a vertex of a stable uncertain VD is the common intersection of three LPGUM bisectors, its envelope has at most six chains. Thus, the complexity of a single stable independent uncertain VD vertex is $O(k)$ and $O(nk)$ for n vertices when the nominal VD is given.

The uncertain VD vertex $v_{ijl}(q) \in V(S(q))$ is computed as follows. Let $l_{ij}(q), l_{jl}(q), l_{li}(q)$ be the three LPGUM bisectors that define the vertex. The upper and lower envelopes of bisector $l_{ij}(q)$ intersect only once with the upper and lower envelopes of bisector $l_{jl}(q)$ (Section 6.4). Thus, computing the intersection of two LPGUM bisectors $l_{ij}(q), l_{jl}(q)$ amounts to computing the four intersections of the two pairs of upper and lower chains.

To compute the intersection of two chains, consider the following procedure. First, rotate the chains so that $\bar{l}_{ij}$ is parallel to the horizontal axis. Next, partition the plane into $O(k)$ zones with vertical lines passing through every endpoint of both chains. Note that the vertical lines intersect both chains: one chain in its endpoint and in the other chain at a new vertex. In this way, the vertical lines partition the plane into $O(k)$ zones. The zones are regions bounded by at least one vertical line and contain two chain segments: one from line $l_{ij}(q)$ and one from line $l_{jl}(q)$. For every zone, we test if the two chain segments of the current zone, one of each line, intersect in $O(k)$ time.

Intersecting the pseudo-square of LPGUM bisectors $l_{ij}(q), l_{jl}(q)$ with the third LPGUM bisector $l_{li}(q)$ is performed in a similar fashion by finding the intersection between the upper and lower envelopes of bisector $l_{li}(q)$ with each edge of the pseudo-square. Since there are four chains in the pseudo-square and two chains of the envelope of LPGUM bisector $l_{li}(q)$, the number of intersections is constant. Thus, computing the intersection between the pseudo-square and LPGUM bisector $l_{li}(q)$ takes $O(k)$ time. Computing all the uncertain vertices of a stable independent uncertain VD takes $O(nk)$ time.   □

6.6.3   Uncertain Voronoi edge computation

The uncertain edges of a stable uncertain VD are LPGUM bisector segments whose endpoints are uncertain VD vertices. Thus, we compute the uncertain edges by first computing the LPGUM bisectors and then intersecting them in triples to obtain the uncertain vertices. Finally, we traverse in sequential incremental order the chains that define the envelopes of uncertain vertices and LPGUM bisectors. The results are the edge uncertainty envelope boundaries. Note that an uncertain VD edge is not an LPGUM edge.

Lemma 6.9. *The complexity of a stable independent uncertain VD edge is $O(k)$ and $O(nk)$ for all n edges. These edges can be computed in $O(nk^2)$ time when the nominal VD is given.*

Proof.   An uncertain edge is defined by an LPGUM bisector and by at most two uncertain vertices. The complexity of an LPGUM bisector and of an uncertain vertex is $O(k)$. Therefore, the complexity of an uncertain edge is $O(k)$, and $O(nk)$ for all edges. Computing the LPGUM bisectors of a stable uncertain VD takes $O(nk^2)$ time. Computing the vertices of an independent VD takes $O(nk)$. Thus, the overall time complexity is $O(nk^2)$. $\qquad\square$

6.6.4 Uncertain Voronoi face computation

The uncertain faces of a stable independent uncertain VD are formed by uncertain edges. Since the uncertain VD is stable, its faces can be computed in a manner similar to the exact VD ones.

Lemma 6.10. *The average complexity of a stable independent uncertain VD face is $O(k)$ and $O(nk)$ for all n faces. They are computed in $O(nk)$ time when the nominal VD, the uncertain vertices and edges are given.*

Proof. Each face of a stable independent uncertain VD consists of chains of uncertain edges and uncertain vertices. The average face of a VD has six edges. Each envelope of uncertain edge and uncertain vertex is defined by $O(k)$ chains — consequently an uncertain face is defined by $O(k)$ chains. The complexity of all uncertain VD faces is $O(nk)$ when the nominal VD is given.

To compute the uncertain faces, we traverse the chain in counterclockwise order, on the interior/exterior of the uncertain edge envelope chain, until we reach an uncertain VD vertex. We repeat this procedure until we return to the starting chain. The next uncertain face is computed similarly. Since the face's complexity is $O(nk)$ and we traverse the chains once, the complexity of the uncertain VD face's computation is $O(nk)$. $\qquad\square$

6.7 Point Location Queries in a Stable Uncertain Voronoi Diagram

We describe next the exact and uncertain LPGUM point location queries in a stable uncertain VD.

6.7.1 Exact point location query

Let p be an exact point and let $VD(S(q)) = (V(S(q)), E(S(q)), F(S(q)))$ be the uncertain VD of LPGUM point set

$S(q) = \{s_1(q), \ldots, s_n(q)\}$. Point p may be inside one or more faces, depending on if it is in an uncertain vertex, in an uncertain edge or in an uncertain face:

Uncertain vertex: when p is inside an uncertain vertex $v_{ijl}(q) \in V(S(q))$, then $\exists q_a, q_b, q_c \in \Delta$ such that $p \in f_i(q_a), p \in f_j(q_b)$, $p \in f_l(q_c)$. Moreover $\exists q_d, q_e, q_f \in \Delta$ such that $p \in e_{ij}(q_d), p \in e_{jl}(q_e), p \in e_{li}(q_f)$ and also $\exists q_g \in \Delta$ such that $p \in v_{ijl}(q_g)$. Thus, point p may be inside faces $f_i(q), f_j(q), f_l(q) \in F(S(q))$.

Uncertain edge: when p is inside an uncertain edge $e_{ij}(q) \in E(S(q))$, then $\exists q_a, q_b \in \Delta$ such that $p \in f_i(q_a), p \in f_j(q_b)$ and also $\exists q_c \in \Delta$ such that $p \in e_{ij}(q_c)$. Thus, point p may be in faces $f_i(q), f_j(q) \in F(S(q))$.

Uncertain face: when p is inside an uncertain face $f_i(q) \in F(S(q))$, then $\forall q_a \in \Delta$ point p placed inside the face $f_i(q_a)$. Thus, point p is inside face $f_i(q)$.

We describe next three methods to answer LPGUM point location queries. The first is based on the nominal VD, the second on the uncertain VD and the third is based on an extended trapezoidal decomposition of the uncertain VD. Table 6.2 summarizes the time and space complexities of the three methods.

6.7.1.1   *Nominal Voronoi diagram*

The first method consists of building the nominal Voronoi diagram $\overline{VD}$ and constructing a trapezoidal map. The trapezoidal map is constructed by extending upward and downward a vertical line from each vertex until it intersects with a nominal segment [62]. We then find the nominal face $\bar{f}_i \in \bar{F}$ in which point p lays. Next, we compute the bisectors that define the uncertain face $f_i(q)$ and for the independent case, we compute the uncertain edges and vertices that define the uncertain face $f_i(q)$. We then test if p coincides with a bisector for the dependent case; for the independent case, we test if p coincides with an uncertain vertex, edge or face. The output depends on the location of p.

The nominal trapezoidal map does not indicate whether the point that is inside a trapezoid should be tested against the edges of this trapezoid only. For some parametric instances, the point can be in a

Table 6.2. Summary of the time and space complexity of three methods for answering exact point location queries in a stable VD. The first two rows apply to both dependent and independent stable VDs.

Case	Method	Preprocessing time	Query time		Space
1	Nominal VD	$O(n \log n)$	**Average case** $O(\log n + k^2)$	**Worst case** $O(nk^2)$	$O(n)$
2	Uncertain VD	$O(nk^2 + n \log n)$	**Average case** $O(\log n + k)$	**Worst case** $O(nk)$	$O(nk)$
3	Extended trapezoidal map Independent case	$O(nk^2 + nk \log n)$	$O(\log n + \log k)$		

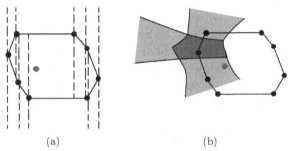

(a)   (b)

Fig. 6.11. Illustration of the worst case for the nominal VD method. The query point is shown in gray; (a) the trapezoidal map is shown as dotted lines. The nominal cell is shown in black solid lines and is defined by the black points; (b) the LPGUM edges and uncertain vertex are shown in gray. The query point lies inside the uncertain edge.

neighbor cell, or on the edge between the two cells. In the worst case, there are $O(n)$ neighbors and the point should be tested according to all of them. Figure 6.11 illustrates this with a simple example.

Complexity: In the preprocessing step, computing the nominal Voronoi diagram $\overline{VD}$ and decomposing it into trapezoidal map takes $O(n \log n)$ time and $O(n)$ space. Finding the nominal face $\bar{f}_i$ in which point p lays takes $O(\log n)$ time. Computing the uncertain edges' vertices (for the dependent case, computing the uncertain bisectors) and finding the uncertain face $f_i(q)$ take on average $O(k^2)$ time since each Voronoi face has on average six neighbors. In the worst case, $O(nk^2)$ time is required.

For the dependent case, testing if p is inside an uncertain vertex, edge or face is performed by traversing in counterclockwise order the segment chains that define the bisectors of uncertain face $f_i(q)$. Each such chain consists of line and parabola segments. For each segment, we test if point p is to the left of the segment. If so, point p is inside face $f_i(q)$, otherwise p is in an uncertain vertex or edge. Since there are $O(k)$ segments in each chain, finding if point p is inside a face takes on average $O(k)$ time and $O(nk)$ in the worst case. Thus, each query takes on average $O(\log n + k^2)$ time and $O(\log n + nk^2)$ in the worst case.

6.7.1.2   *Uncertain Voronoi diagram*

The second method consists of computing the nominal Voronoi diagram $\overline{VD}$, constructing a trapezoidal map, and then computing its uncertain Voronoi diagram $VD(S(q))$ for the independent case, or all the uncertain bisectors for the dependent case. The preprocessing takes $O(nk^2 + n \log n)$ time and $O(nk)$ space. Each query requires on average $O(\log n + k)$ time and $O(nk)$ in the worst case. This method applies to both the independent and the dependent cases.

6.7.1.3   *Extended trapezoidal map (Independent case)*

The third method is applicable to the independent case only because the problem of computing the uncertain vertex of a dependent VD is open. It consists of building the independent stable Voronoi diagram $VD(S(q))$ and computing its trapezoidal map. An independent stable uncertain VD consists of line and parabola segments. However, the standard trapezoidal map method is defined for nominal line segments: The construction and search are performed by testing if a point lies on, left or right of a vertical line and if a point lies on, above or below a segment. The trapezoidal map can be directly extended to parabola segments as follows. When the parabola segment is x-monotone, we test if the query point lies on, above or below the parabola in constant time. Otherwise, we introduce a vertical line that is tangent to the parabola, thereby splitting it into two x-monotone parabola segments, each of which is tested as described above.

Since there are $O(nk)$ parabolas that are not x-monotone, and each parabola is extended with one vertical tangent line, the total number of vertices, the line segments and parabola segments remains $O(nk)$. Since there are $O(nk)$ vertices in an independent stable VD, the space complexity of the search structure is $O(nk)$. It takes $O(nk^2)$ time to build the independent VD and $O(nk \log nk)$ to decompose the diagram, and thus the overall time is $O(nk^2 + nk \log nk) = O(nk^2 + nk \log n)$. Each query takes $O(\log nk) = O(\log n + \log k)$ time.

6.7.2   Uncertain point location query

The three types of uncertain point location queries in an uncertain Voronoi diagram $VD(S(q))$ are

Type 1: Determine if uncertain point $u(q)$ is **always fully contained** in a single face of an uncertain VD.

Type 2: List the faces of the uncertain VD that **may contain** uncertain point $u(q)$.

Type 3: Compute the faces of the uncertain VD that **may contain** uncertain point $u(q)$.

For Type 1 queries, we compute the uncertainty zone of point $u(q)$ and choose one of the vertices that defines $u(q)$, e.g., the first one, $p_1 \in U = \langle p_1, \ldots, p_k \rangle$. Next, we find in which face/faces the exact point p_1 is with one of the methods described in Section 6.7.1. If point p_1 is in more than one face, then the output of the query is false. Otherwise, if point p_1 is inside face $f_i(q)$, we test if $u(q)$ is fully contained in uncertain face $f_i(q)$. The dependent and independent cases are each handled as follows.

Independent case: since an uncertain VD face forms a polygon whose edges are chains and the uncertainty zone of an LPGUM point is bounded by a zonotope, we use a standard algorithm for the intersection of polygonal chains [62]. When LPGUM point $u(q)$ is fully contained in uncertain face $f_i(q)$, the output is *true, false* otherwise.

Dependent case: for each LPGUM bisector that is part of $f_i(q)$, we choose two different LPGUM points that lie on it, $v(q)$ and $w(q)$, and test if there is an orientation flip between LPGUM points $u(q), v(q), w(q)$ with the method described in Section 3.2. If there is an orientation flip, then point $u(q)$ is not fully contained in uncertain face $f_i(q)$ and the output is *false*, *true* otherwise.

The time complexity of the query is as follows. Computing the uncertainty zone of an LPGUM point takes $O(k \log k)$ time. Finding in which face/faces p_1 lies on depends on which method in Section 6.7.1 is used. For the independent case, we test if $u(q)$ is fully contained in an uncertain face, which requires $O(k)$ time on average and $O(nk)$ time in the worst case. For the dependent case, an orientation flip among three LPGUM points can be detected in $O(k^2)$ time (Section 3.2). On average, a constant number of orientation flips is performed, and $O(n)$ in the worst case. Thus, the overall the time complexity is $O(k^2)$ and $O(nk^2)$ for the average and worst cases, respectively.

Table 6.3 (top) summarizes the complexity of three methods for the uncertain point query in the independent case. The uncertain VD and the extended trapezoidal map query methods have the same query and space complexity. However, the preprocessing time complexity of the latter has a lower time complexity, so it is the preferred one. The nominal VD method has a better preprocessing and space complexity; however, each query has a higher time complexity.

Table 6.3 (bottom) summarizes the complexity of the query for the dependent case. The nominal VD and the uncertain VD methods have the same query time complexity. The nominal VD method has a better space and preprocessing time complexity. For Type 2 queries, let t be the number of uncertain faces that LPGUM point $u(q)$ may lay inside them. First, we compute the uncertainty zone of point $u(q)$ and choose one of the vertices that defines $u(q)$, e.g., the first one: $p_1 \in U = \langle p_1, \ldots, p_k \rangle$. Next, we find in which face exact point p_1 is with one of the methods in Section 6.7.1. Then, we process the dependent and independent cases as follows.

Independent case: We find the intersection points of $u(q)$ and the uncertain face in constant time for each point and proceed to the next uncertain face in which $u(q)$ may be. We repeat this process for adjacent faces until we return to the starting point to find all the uncertain faces that intersect with $u(q)$. Finally, we find all the uncertain faces that contain $u(q)$ by traversing the uncertain edges of the faces that intersect $u(q)$ and then traversing the inner faces that contain $u(q)$ until we return to the faces that were already found.

Table 6.3. Summary of the time and space complexity of three approaches for LPGUM point location queries in an independent (top) and dependent (bottom) stable Voronoi diagram.

Independent case

Type	Method	Preprocessing time	Query time		Space
			Average case	Worst case	
1	Nominal Voronoi diagram	$O(n\log n)$	$O(\log n + k^2)$	$O(nk^2)$	$O(n)$
2	Uncertain Voronoi diagram	$O(nk^2 + n\log n)$	$O(\log n + k\log k)$	$O(nk + k\log k)$	$O(nk)$
3	Extended trapezoidal map	$O(nk^2 + nk\log n)$			

Dependent case

Type	Method	Preprocessing time	Query time		Space
			Average case	Worst case	
1	Nominal Voronoi diagram	$O(n\log n + k\log k)$	$O(\log n + k^2)$	$O(nk^2)$	$O(n)$
2	Uncertain Voronoi diagram	$O(nk^2 + n\log n)$	$O(\log n + k^2)$	$O(nk^2)$	$O(nk)$

Dependent case: For each LPGUM bisector of $f_i(q)$, we select two LPGUM points on it, $v(q)$ and $w(q)$. If there is an orientation flip between LPGUM points $u(q), v(q), w(q)$, then point $u(q)$ is not fully contained in uncertain face $f_i(q)$ and may be inside the neighbor uncertain face $f_j(q)$. Similarly, we test each LPGUM bisector that forms $f_j(q)$ until we find all the uncertain faces that may contain LPGUM point $u(q)$.

The time complexity of these methods is similar to that of Type 1 queries with the following additions. For the independent case, traversing an uncertain face takes on average $O(k)$ time and $O(nk)$ in the worst case. When there are t uncertain faces in $VD(S(q))$ that may contain LPGUM point $u(q)$, the overall time complexity of traversing and finding the intersections is $O(tk)$ on average and $O(nk)$ in the worst case. Thus, the time complexity is the same. On average, an extra $O(tk)$ time is required for each query.

For the dependent case, first we traverse the bisector edges of each face and test for orientation flip. The complexity for the average case is $O(tk^2)$ and $O(nk^2)$ for the worst case. Thus, the time complexity of the Type 1 and 2 queries is the same. The only difference is an addition of $O(tk^2)$ time to the average case of each query.

Type 3 queries are useful for statistical queries, e.g., to compute the probability that LPGUM point $u(q)$ is inside a face. For the independent case, the algorithm is similar to the one for Type 2 queries. The difference is that we compute the uncertain faces that intersect with LPGUM point $u(q)$ so that the new boundary of the uncertain face is formed by parts of the envelope of $u(q)$. Thus, the time complexity of the Type 1 and 2 queries is the same, with the addition of $O(tk)$ time to the average case.

Note that the algorithm for subdivision intersection can also be applied to answer Type 3 queries. Computing the uncertain VD takes $O(nk^2 + n \log n)$ time; computing $u(q)$ takes $O(k \log k)$ time; computing the subdivision intersection takes $O(nk \log nk)$. Overall, the complexity is $O(nk^2 + n \log n + nk \log k + nk \log n) = O(nk^2 + nk \log n)$. Note that this algorithm has a higher time complexity than the previous one. Note also that the overlay of two planar subdivisions of complexity n can be computed in $O(n \log n + t \log n)$ where t is the complexity of the resulting overlay [62].

For the dependent case, to compute the faces of $VD(S(q))$ that may contain LPGUM point $u(q)$, we have to compute the uncertainty zone of the intersection between an uncertain face and an LPGUM point, between three LPGUM lines (uncertain vertex), between an uncertain vertex and an LPGUM point and between an LPGUM line and an LPGUM point. These remain open problems. The algorithm for answering this query is the same as that of the independent case.

6.8 Dynamic Stable Uncertain Voronoi Diagram

We now describe how to efficiently update a stable uncertain Voronoi diagram $VD(S(q))$ by inserting or deleting an LPGUM point.

Insertion: The addition of a new LPGUM point $v(q)$ to $VD(S(q))$ may result in an unstable uncertain VD. We thus determine first if $VD(S(q) \cup \{v(q)\})$ is stable and if so, update $VD(S(q))$. Then, we find the face in the nominal VD that contains $\bar{v}$ in $O(\log n)$ time. Next, we update the nominal vicinity of $\bar{v}$ in constant time on average and in $O(n)$ time in the worst case. We perform an in-circle test in $O(k \log k)$ time for the independent case and $O(P_4(k))$ time for the dependent case, where $P_4(k)$ is the complexity of quartic k-variable optimization. There are six in-circle tests in the average case and $O(n)$ in the worst case. Updating the uncertain VD takes $O(k^2)$ in the average case and $O(nk^2)$ in the worst case. Overall, the point insertion takes $O(k^2 + \log n)$ and $O(nk^2 + \log n)$ in the average and worst cases for the independent case and $O(k^2 + \log n + P_4(k))$ and $O(nk^2 + nP_4(k))$ in the average and worst cases for the dependent case.

Deletion: The deletion of LPGUM point $v(q)$ from $VD(S(q))$ may also result in an unstable uncertain Voronoi diagram $VD(S(q) - \{v(q)\})$. We thus determine first if $VD(S(q) - \{v(q)\})$ is stable and if so, update $VD(S(q))$. For the stability test, consider the nominal Voronoi diagram $\overline{VD}$. We first compute the face in which $\bar{v}$ lies, delete $\bar{v}$ from $\overline{VD}$ and then update its neighboring faces [77]. The stability tests are the same as for the insertion because the nominal faces that are affected by the deletion are the same as those of the insertion. To see this, consider the nominal VD: Remove one point and then add it as described in [77]. Since the VD remains unchanged, the faces affected by the deletion and the insertion are the same. When all the in-circle tests of the affected points are negative, we update the uncertain edges and vertices to obtain the updated nominal VD. The time complexity of deletion is the same as the one for insertion.

6.9 Summary

This chapter addresses problems related to the construction of the VD and DT of a set of LPGUM points in the plane with mutually dependent location uncertainties. The contributions of this chapter are as follows: (1) the formulation of the uncertain VD and DT problems in the LPGUM for both dependent and independent point location uncertainties and the derivation of their basic properties; (2) the first $O(nP_4(k))$ uncertain VD stability test algorithm for the dependent case, where $P_4(k)$ is the complexity of quartic k-variable optimization when the nominal VD is given; (3) a new $O(nk \log k)$ time stability test algorithm for the independent case when the nominal (exact) VD is given; (4) a proof that an unstable VD may have an exponential number of topologically different instances; (5) new algorithms to compute the vertices, edges and faces of an uncertain VD for the independent case whose complexity is $O(nk^2 + n \log n)$ time and $O(nk)$ space; (6) algorithms for answering point location queries in a stable uncertain VD and for dynamically updating an uncertain VD in $O(k^2 + \log n + P_4(k))$ and $O(k^2 + \log n)$ and average case time complexity for the dependent and independent cases.

Chapter 7

Conclusion

This chapter concludes the book and presents several open problems.

7.1 Summary

This book introduces the Linear Parametric Geometric Uncertainty Model (LPGUM), which is to the best of our knowledge the first model for handling geometric uncertainty with dependencies. Within LPGUM, we conducted a systematic investigation of some of the basic problems in Computational Geometry.

Below, we list the problems we have solved as well as open problems and possible directions for future research. The problems we have solved range from the most basic problems of computing and describing a point, line and three-point circle through half-plane point retrieval queries, to more elaborate problems including EMST, Voronoi diagram and Delaunay triangulation of a set of uncertain LPGUM points. Solving this variety of problems demonstrates that LPGUM is an expressive and computationally viable model for representing and computing with geometric dependent uncertainties.

This book provides a general and efficient model to facilitate geometric computation with imprecise data. In particular, the model and algorithms provide the following:

1. A worst-case analysis of dependent uncertainties.
2. A complete characterization of the geometric uncertainty.

3. An explicit representation of the dependencies between uncertainties.
4. A low computational time increase for incorporating uncertainties.

The model and algorithms described in this book meet these goals. Chapter 2 describes LPGUM, a parametric model for modeling geometric uncertainty that allows for dependencies among objects. Chapter 3 presents a complete characterization of the worst-case analysis of coordinates, points, lines and three-point circles under LPGUM and shows that they can be computed in low polygonal time and space. Chapters 4–6 demonstrate that LPGUM can be used in solving classical computational geometry problems while allowing the objects to entail uncertainty.

The linear parametric geometric uncertainty model

The LPGUM provides an effective means for modeling uncertain geometric objects with parametric dependencies. To make this model useful in a variety of fields, an automated method for generating a parametric model is needed. We suggest that for key fields and practical problems, e.g., CAD/CAM and robotics, specific automated methods for transforming the existing models to LPGUM be devised.

The contributions of this book as are follows.

The envelope of points, lines and circles: We have presented algorithms for computing the uncertainty envelope of LPGUM points, lines and three-point circles in the plane and have provided a complete description of their geometric properties. We have proven that the geometric complexity of an LPGUM line envelope in the plane is $O(k)$ and have described an $O(k^2)$ algorithm for computing it. Also, we have proven that the geometric complexity of an independent LPGUM three-point circle envelope in the plane is $O(1)$ and have described an $O(k \log k)$ algorithm for computing it.

Half-plane point retrieval queries: We have defined a family of geometric half-plane retrieval queries of points in the plane in the presence of geometric uncertainty in LPGUM and have described efficient algorithms to answer them. The problems include exact and uncertain point sets and half-plane queries defined by an exact or uncertain line whose location uncertainties are independent or dependent and are defined by k real-valued parameters. We classify the points into three disjoint sets: ABOVE, BELOW and UNCERT. We describe both one-shot and recurrent algorithms for half-plane queries.

Euclidean minimum spanning trees: We have defined the uncertain EMST stability of a set of LPGUM points modeled with real-valued uncertainty parameters. We proved that when the uncertain EMST is unstable, it may have an exponential number of topologically different instances, thus precluding its polynomial time computation. We have presented algorithms for comparing two edge weights defined by the distance between the edge endpoints. We described an uncertain EMST stability test algorithm and a method for computing its minimum and maximum total weight.

Voronoi diagram and Delaunay triangulation: We addressed the problems related to the construction of the Voronoi diagram and Delaunay triangulation of a set of points in the plane with dependent location uncertainties. We proved that when the uncertain VD is unstable, it may have an exponential number of topological different instances, thus precluding its polynomial time computation. We have presented an uncertain VD stability test algorithm and have described algorithms to compute the vertices, edges and faces of an uncertain Voronoi diagram for the independent case and algorithms for answering point location queries in a stable uncertain Voronoi diagram and for dynamically updating an uncertain Voronoi diagram.

7.2 Open Problems

One limitation of the LPGUM model is that the parameter uncertainty intervals are independent of each other. That is, although under LPGUM many objects may depend on a common set of parameters and thus the objects are interdependent, variations in the value of one parameter do not affect the value of other parameters. When there are dependencies among *parameter intervals*, the uncertainty domain is not a hypercube, and thus the algorithms presented in this book are no longer applicable. The problem of formulating and solving geometric problems with such a model is open.

Several open problems warrant further investigation. These include improving the time complexity of the line envelope computation or showing that $O(k^2)$ is a lower bound. Other extensions include uncertain triangle and polygon queries in the LPGUM model. Other open problems include developing efficient algorithms for comparing two edge weights for the dependent case, determining the lower bound complexity of the uncertain EMST stability testing, testing for partial stability of an uncertain EMST and exploring the connection between uncertain EMSTs and Voronoi diagrams in LPGUM. Further open problems include improving the time complexity of the in-circle test for the dependent case and developing an algorithm to compute the intersection of three dependent LPGUM lines. The solutions to these problems will directly improve the time complexity bounds of the uncertain Voronoi and Delaunay triangulation stability testing and computation. Additional research directions include the large variety of problems that are related to Voronoi diagrams, e.g., uncertain furthest Voronoi diagram, kth order Voronoi diagrams and weighted Voronoi diagrams in the LPGUM.

Natural extensions include defining and deriving the properties of more complex geometric objects, i.e., splines, conics and other types of curves in LPGUM, and developing algorithms for computing their envelopes. Exploring the LPGUM of elementary geometric objects with dependent geometric uncertainties in 3D space is also of great importance.

References

1. de Berg, M., Mumford, E., Roeloffzen, M. (2010) Finding structures on imprecise points. *Proc. 26th European Workshop on Computational Geometry*, pp. 85–88.
2. Javad, A., Mohades, A., Davoodi, M., Sheikhi, F. (2010) Convex hull of imprecise points modeled by segments. *Proc. 26th European Workshop on Computational Geometry*, pp. 193–196.
3. Löffler, M., van Kreveld, M. (2010) Largest and smallest convex hulls for imprecise points. *Algorithmica* 56(2):235–245.
4. Löffler, M., van Kreveld, M. (2010) Largest bounding box, smallest diameter, and related problems on imprecise points. *Computational Geometry* 43(4):419–433.
5. McAllister, M., Kirkpatrick, D., Snoeyink, J. (1996) A compact piecewise linear Voronoi diagram for convex sites in the plane. *Discrete & Computational Geometry* 15(1):73–105.
6. Sember, J. (2011) Guarantees concerning geometric objects with imprecise points. Doctoral dissertation, University of British Columbia.
7. Jooyandeh, M., Mohades A., Mirzakhah, M. (2009) Uncertain Voronoi diagram. *Information Processing Letters* 109(13):709–712.
8. Luo, C., Franciosa, P., Mo Z., Ceglarek, D. (2020) A framework for tolerance modeling based on parametric space envelope. *Journal of Manufacturing Science and Engineering* 142:1014.
9. Weller, F. (1997) Stability of Voronoi neighborship under perturbations of the sites. *Proc. 9th Canadian Conference on Computational Geometry*, pp. 251–256.
10. Guibas, L. J., Salesin, D., Stolfi, J. (1989) Epsilon geometry: Building robust algorithms from imprecise computations. *Proc. 5th Annual ACM Symposium on Computational Geometry*, pp. 208–217.

11. Guibas, L. J., Salesin, D., Stolfi, J. (1993) Constructing strongly convex approximate hulls with inaccurate primitives. *Algorithmica* 9:534–560.
12. Du Plessis, A., Wall, C. T. C. (1995) *The Geometry of Topological Stability*. Clarendon Press, Oxford, UK.
13. Arya, S., Mount, D. M. (2000) Approximate range searching. *Computational Geometry* 17(3–4):135–152.
14. Pfoser, D., Jensen, C. S. (1999) Capturing the uncertainty of moving-object representations. *Proc. Int. Symposium on Spatial Databases*. pp. 111–131. Springer, Berlin, Heidelberg.
15. Trajcevski, G. (2003) Probabilistic range queries in moving objects databases with uncertainty. *Proc. 3rd ACM Int. Workshop on Data Engineering for Wireless and Mobile Access*, pp. 39–45.
16. Ben-Tal, A., El Ghaoui, L., Nemirovski, A. (2009) *Robust Optimization*. Princeton University Press, Princeton, USA.
17. Löffler, M., Snoeyink, J. (2008) Delaunay triangulations of imprecise points in linear time after preprocessing. *Proc. 24th Annual Symposium on Computational Geometry*, pp. 298–304.
18. Devillers, O. (2011) Delaunay triangulation of imprecise points, pre-process and actually get a fast query time. *Journal of Computational Geometry* 2(1):30–45.
19. Buchin, K., Löffler, M., Morin P., Mulzer, W. (2011) Preprocessing imprecise points for Delaunay triangulation: Simplified and extended. *Algorithmica* 61(3):674–693.
20. Cheng, R., Xia, Y., Prabhakar, S., Shah, R., Vitter, J. S. (2004) Efficient indexing methods for probabilistic threshold queries over uncertain data. *Proc. 13th Int. Conf. on Very Large Data Bases VLDB Endowment*. Vol. 30, pp. 876–887.
21. Chen, J., Cheng, R. (2007) Efficient evaluation of imprecise location-dependent queries. *Proc. 23rd IEEE Int. Conf. on Data Engineering*, pp. 586–595.
22. Agarwal, P. K., Cheng, S. W., Tao, Y., Yi, K. (2009) Indexing uncertain data. *Proc. 28th ACM SIGMOD-SIGACT-SIGART Symposium on Principles of Database Systems*, pp. 137–146.
23. Kamousi, P., Chan, T. M., Suri, S. (2011) Closest pair and the post office problem for stochastic points. *Proc. Workshop on Algorithms and Data Structures*, pp. 548–559.
24. Kamousi, P., Chan, T. M., Suri, S. (2011) Stochastic minimum spanning trees in Euclidean spaces. *Proc. 27th ACM Annual Symposium on Computational Geometry*, pp. 65–74.
25. Fink, M., Hershberger, J., Kumar, N., Suri, S. (2016). Hyperplane separability and convexity of probabilistic point sets. *Proc. 32nd Int. Symp. on Computational Geometry*, 38:1–38:16. Schloss Dagstuhl, Dagstuhl, Germany.

26. Xue, J., Li, Y. (2016) Colored stochastic dominance problems. arXiv preprint arXiv:1612.06954.

27. Agarwal, P. K., Har-Peled, S., Suri, S., Yıldız, H., Zhang, W. (2017) Convex hulls under uncertainty. *Algorithmica* 79(2):340–367.

28. Suri, S., Verbeek, K., Yıldız, H. (2013) On the most likely convex hull of uncertain points. *Proc. European Symposium on Algorithms*, pp. 791–802.

29. Pérez-Lantero, P. (2016) Area and perimeter of the convex hull of stochastic points. *The Computer Journal* 59(8):1144–1154.

30. Jaromczyk, J. W., Wasilkowski, G. W. (1994) Computing convex hull in a floating point arithmetic. *Computational Geometry* 4(5):283–292.

31. Fortune, S. (1989) Stable maintenance of point set triangulations in two dimensions. *Proc. 54th Annual Symposium on Foundations of Computer Science*, pp. 494–499.

32. Fortune, S. (1992) Numerical stability of algorithms for 2D Delaunay triangulations. *Proc. 8th Annual Symposium on Computational Geometry*, pp. 83–92.

33. Ely, J. S., Leclerc, A. P. (2000) Correct Delaunay triangulation in the presence of inexact inputs and arithmetic. *Reliable Computing* 6(1): 23–38.

34. Abellanas, M., Hurtado, F., Ramos, P. A. (1999) Structural tolerance and Delaunay triangulation. *Information Processing Letters* 71(5): 221–227.

35. Boissonnat, J. D., Dyer, R., Ghosh, A. (2013) The stability of Delaunay triangulations. *International Journal of Computational Geometry & Applications* 23(4–5):303–333.

36. Li, Z., Milenkovic, V. (1992) Constructing strongly convex hulls using exact or rounded arithmetic. *Algorithmica* 8(1–6):345–364.

37. Evans, W., Sember, J. (2008) Guaranteed Voronoi diagrams of uncertain sites. *Proc. 20th Canadian Conference on Computational Geometry*, pp. 207–210.

38. Reem, D. (2011) The geometric stability of Voronoi diagrams with respect to small changes of the sites. *Proc. 27th Annual Symposium on Computational Geometry*, pp. 254–263.

39. Goberna, M., de Serio, V. V. (2012) On the stability of Voronoi cells. *TOP: Ocial Journal of the Spanish Society of Statistics and Operations Research* 20(2):411–425.

40. Meulemans, W., Speckmann, B., Verbeek, K., Wulms, J. (2018) A framework for algorithm stability and its application to kinetic Euclidean MSTs. *Proc. Latin American Symposium on Theoretical Informatics*, pp. 805–819. Springer, Cham.

41. Agarwal, P. K., Gao, J., Guibas, L. J., Kaplan, H., Koltun, V., Rubin, N., Sharir, M. (2010) Kinetic stable Delaunay graphs. *Proc. 26th Annual Symp. on Computational Geometry*, pp. 127–136.

42. Agarwal, P. K., Gao, J., Guibas, L. J., Kaplan, H., Rubin, N., Sharir, M. (2015) Stable Delaunay graphs. *Discrete & Computational Geometry* 54(4):905–929.

43. Albers, G., Guibas, L. J., Mitchell J. S., Roos, T. (1998) Voronoi diagrams of moving points. *International Journal of Computational Geometry & Applications* 8(3):365–379.

44. Xie, X., Cheng, R., Yiu, M. L., Sun, L., Chen, J. (2013) UV-diagram: A Voronoi diagram for uncertain spatial databases. *The VLDB Journal* 22(3):319–344.

45. Iijima, Y., Ishikawa, Y. (2009) Finding probabilistic nearest neighbors for query objects with imprecise locations. *Proc. 10th Int. Conf. of Mobile Data Management: Systems, Services and Middleware*, pp. 52–61.

46. Ali, M. E., Tanin, E., Zhang R., Kotagiri, R. (2012) Probabilistic Voronoi diagrams for probabilistic moving nearest neighbor queries. *Data & Knowledge Engineering* 75:1–33.

47. Arya, S., Malamatos, T., Mount, D. M. (2002) Space-efficient approximate Voronoi diagrams. *Proc. 34th Annual ACM Symposium on Theory of Computing*, pp. 721–730.

48. Suri, S., Verbeek, K. (2016) On the most likely Voronoi diagram and nearest neighbor searching. *International Journal of Computational Geometry & Applications* 26(3–4):151–166.

49. Joskowicz, L., Myers, Y. (2014) Topological stability and convex hull with dependent uncertainties. *Proc. 30th European Workshop Computational Geometry*, pp. 37–41.

50. Joskowicz, L., Ostrovsky-Berman, Y. (2005) Tolerance envelopes of planar mechanical parts with parametric tolerances. *Computer-Aided Design* 37(5):531–544.

51. Joskowicz, L., Ostrovsky-Berman, Y., Myers, Y. (2010) Efficient representation and computation of geometric uncertainty: The linear parametric model. *Precision Engineering* 34(1):2–6.

52. Myers, Y., Joskowicz, L. (2010) Uncertain geometry with dependencies. *Proc. 14th ACM Symposium on Solid and Physical Modeling*, pp. 159–164.

53. Myers, Y., Joskowicz, L. (2012) Point set distance and orthogonal range problems with dependent geometric uncertainties. *International Journal of Computational Geometry & Applications* 22(6):517–541.

54. Myers, Y., Joskowicz, L. (2013) Uncertain lines and circles with dependencies. *Computer-Aided Design* 45(2):556–561.

55. Ostrovsky-Berman, Y., Joskowicz, L. (2005) Tolerance envelopes of planar mechanical parts with parametric tolerances. *Computer-Aided Design* 37(5):531–544.
56. Gitik, R, Bartal, O., Joskowicz, L. (2021) Euclidean minimum spanning tree with dependent uncertainties. *Computational Geometry: Theory and Applications* 9:10744.
57. Nasson, M. A. (1999) Mathematical definition of dimensioning and tolerancing principles. In: P. J. Drake (ed.), *Dimensioning and Tolerancing Handbook*, McGraw Hill, New York, USA, pp. 7/1–7/15.
58. Balaban, I. J. (1995) An optimal algorithm for finding segments intersections. *Proc. of the 11th Annual Symposium on Computational Geometry*, pp. 211–219.
59. Goodman, J. E. (2004) Pseudoline Arrangements. In: J. E. Goodman, J. O'Rourke (ed.), *Handbook of Discrete and Computational Geometry*, Chapman & Hall/CRC, Boca Raton, USA, pp. 97–128.
60. Chazelle, B., Guibas, L. J., Lee, D. T. (1985) The power of geometric duality. *BIT Numerical Mathematics* 25(1):76–90.
61. Cole, R., Yap, C. K. (1984) Geometric retrieval problems. *Information and Control* 63(1–2):39–57.
62. Van Kreveld, M., Schwarzkopf, O., de Berg, M., Overmars, M. (2000) *Computational Geometry Algorithms and Applications*. Springer, Berlin, Heidelberg, Germany.
63. Agarwal, P. K., Erickson, J. (1999) Geometric range searching and its relatives. *Contemporary Mathematics* 223:1–56.
64. Welzl, E. (1988) Partition trees for triangle counting and other range searching problems. *Proc. 4th Annual Symposium on Computational Geometry*, pp. 23–33.
65. Willard, D. E. (1982) Polygon retrieval. *SIAM Journal on Computing* 11(1):149–165.
66. Edelsbrunner, H., Welzl, E. (1986) Half-planar range search in linear space and $O(n0.695)$ query time. *Information Processing Letters* 23(5):289–293.
67. Chazelle, B., Edelsbrunner, H. (1985) Optimal solutions for a class of point retrieval problems. *Journal of Symbolic Computation* 1(1):47–56.
68. Aron, I. D., Van Hentenryck, P. (2004) On the complexity of the robust spanning tree problem with interval data. *Operations Research Letters* 32(1):36–40.
69. Dorrigiv, R., Fraser, R., He, M., Kamali, S., Kawamura, A., López-Ortiz, A., Seco, D. (2015) On minimum- and maximum-weight minimum spanning trees with neighborhoods. *Theory of Computing Systems* 56(1):220–250.

70. Yang, Y., Lin, M., Xu, J., Xie, Y. (2007) Minimum spanning tree with neighborhoods. *Proc. Int. Conf. on Algorithmic Applications in Management*, pp. 306–316. Springer, Berlin, Heidelberg.

71. Agarwal, P. K., Eppstein, D., Guibas, L. J., Henzinger, M. R. (1998) Parametric and kinetic minimum spanning trees. *Proc. 39th Annual Symposium on Foundations of Computer Science*, pp. 596–605.

72. Ye, Y. (1997) Approximating quadratic programming with bound constraints. *Mathematical Programming* 84:219–226.

73. Hagerup, T. (2009) An even simpler linear-time algorithm for verifying minimum spanning trees. *Proc. Int. Workshop on Graph-Theoretic Concepts in Computer Science*, pp. 178–189. Springer, Berlin, Heidelberg.

74. Lobo, M. S., Vandenberghe, L., Boyd, S., Lebret, H. (1998) Applications of second-order cone programming. *Linear Algebra and Its Applications* 284(1–3):193–228.

75. Lasserre, J. B. (2001) Global optimization with polynomials and the problem of moments. *SIAM Journal on Optimization* 11(3):796–817.

76. Parrilo, P. A. (2003) Semidefinite programming relaxations for semialgebraic problems. *Mathematical Programming* 96(2):293–320.

77. Devillers, O. (2011) Vertex removal in two dimensional Delaunay triangulation: Speedup by low degree optimization. *Computational Geometry* 44:169–177.

Index

Printed in the United States
by Baker & Taylor Publisher Services